Three Sixteen - Unveiling the Heart of God

Three Sixteen - Unveiling the Heart of God

Thomas Carl Rende

To my wife, Pam, who is my rock and my prayer warrior!!

Copyright © 2025 by Thomas Rende
All rights reserved. No part of this book may be reproduced in any manner whatsoever without written permission except in the case of brief quotations embodied in critical articles and reviews.
First Printing, 2025

Introduction

Welcome to "Three Sixteen - Unveiling the Heart of God." In this comprehensive Bible study, we will explore the profound significance of every 3:16 verse in the New Testament. From the Gospels to Paul's epistles and the visions in Revelation, these verses offer deep insights into key themes, theological truths, and practical applications that have resonated with believers for generations.

The decision to focus on the 3:16 verses is deliberate, as each one contains unique treasures waiting to be discovered. Whether it's John 3:16, famously known as the "Gospel in a nutshell," or lesser-known verses like Romans 3:16 or Revelation 3:16, each passage contributes to our understanding of God's character, His redemptive plan, and our role as His followers. Through careful study and reflection, we will uncover the rich layers of meaning embedded within these verses and draw out their relevance for our lives today. Join us as we journey through the New Testament, exploring the profound truths within the 3:16 verses and discovering how they continue to shape and transform the lives of believers around the world.

You'll notice that there are some books in the New Testament that do not have a 3:16 verse. I've included these to create a more complete study experience. They are no less rich in relevance and importance in our lives as the books that have this particular verse. All 27 books will have a study lesson.

I encourage you not just to read each 3:16 verse but to commit it to memory. We are called to hide Scripture in our hearts, and this study provides a set of verses that will fill your heart with understanding, application, and the joy that only Scripture can bring. Additionally, I suggest "reading around the verse," taking in the surrounding context to deepen your understanding of why each writer was led to pen that specific verse. Additionally, you'll need a separate notebook for this study. The questions are designed to prompt personal reflection and allow the Spirit to inspire your thoughts as you write.

Finally, if you choose to read this Bible study as a small group, there are ten small group questions per chapter in the Section Two.

Contents

Section One

Chapter 1 - Matthew 3:16..........................1
Chapter 2 - Mark 3:16................................5
Chapter 3 - Luke 3:16................................9
Chapter 4 - John 3:16..............................13
Chapter 5 - Acts 3:16..............................17
Chapter 6 - Romans 3:16........................21
Chapter 7 - 1 Corinthians 3:16.................25
Chapter 8 - 2 Corinthians 3:16.................31
Chapter 9 - Galatians 3:16......................37
Chapter 10 Ephesians 3:16.....................41
Chapter 11 - Philippians 3:16..................47
Chapter 12 - Colossians 3:16..................53
Chapter 13 - 1 Thessalonians..................57
Chapter 14 - 2 Thessalonians 3:16..........61
Chapter 15 - 1 Timothy 3:16....................65
Chapter 16 - 2 Timothy 3:16....................69
Chapter 17 - Titus 73
Chapter 18 - Philemon............................77
Chapter 19 - Hebrews 3:16......................81
Chapter 20 - James 3:16.........................85
Chapter 21 - 1 Peter 3:16........................89
Chapter 22 - 2 Peter 3:16........................93
Chapter 23 - 1 John 3:16........................97

CONTENTS

Chapter 24 - 2 John..............................101
Chapter 25 - 3 John..............................105
Chapter 26 - Jude.................................109
Chapter 27 - Revelation 3:16..................115

Section Two

Discussion Questions........................121

Section One

"The very practice of reading [the Bible] will have a purifying effect upon your mind and heart. Let nothing take the place of this daily exercise."

Billy Graham

"We come to Scripture not to learn a subject but to steep ourselves in a person."

C. S. Lewis

Matthew 3:16

Picture the scene in Matthew 3:13-17: the sun is high, casting shadows across the rocky landscape as Jesus approaches the Jordan River along a dusty path. The air is filled with the sound of moving water and the quiet murmurs of people nearby. Standing waist-deep in the river is John the Baptist, strong-voiced, baptizing those who seek repentance and a fresh start. Jesus, blending into the crowd, waits patiently, knowing this moment will mark the beginning of His journey toward the cross and fulfilling His mission.

But why does Jesus, sinless and the Son of God, come to be baptized? Many have wondered why the one who came to save humanity would do this. When John questions Him, Jesus answers, "Let it be so now; it is proper for us to do this to fulfill all righteousness." Jesus' choice to be baptized is more than a symbolic act—it's His way of fully identifying with humanity. He steps into the same waters as those who seek repentance, showing His commitment to His mission.

The Jewish people expected a warrior Messiah who would free them, but here stands Jesus, not on a battlefield but humbly at the river, asking to be baptized. Jesus shows strength and dedication, setting an example by embracing His role with humility.

In Matthew 3:13-15, there's a moment of humility between Jesus and John. John hesitates, feeling unworthy to baptize Jesus. John's protest isn't pride but deep respect for who Jesus is. Yet, Jesus gently insists, assuring John that this is necessary. By being baptized, Jesus fulfills the prophecy in Isaiah 53:11, identifying with the humanity He came to save.

John agrees, understanding that this act is part of God's divine plan. Jesus's baptism isn't a routine ritual; it launches His public ministry, showing humility and obedience that He calls all His followers to live out. This baptism begins His mission to bring hope and salvation to everyone who believes.

As Jesus rises from the water in Matthew 3:16, a remarkable thing happens. The heavens open, and the Holy Spirit descends upon Him like a dove. This moment is rich with symbolism, especially for a Jewish audience familiar with how God's Spirit came upon kings like Saul (1 Samuel 10:6) and David (1 Samuel 16:13). Here, God anoints Jesus not as a warrior-king but as the compassionate, loving King of all people.

The dove's descent shows the Holy Spirit's vital role in Jesus's work. It recalls the dove in Genesis that returned to Noah with an olive branch, marking the start of a new world (Genesis 8:11-12). Similarly, the Spirit's arrival marks the beginning of a new era through Jesus, the "Prince of Peace" (Isaiah 9:6), who will bring peace to the world.

Then, in Matthew 3:17, a voice from heaven declares, "This is my beloved Son, with whom I am well pleased." These words echo Isaiah 42:1, where God is pleased with His chosen servant who will bring justice to the nations. These words also remind us of Psalm 2:7, "You are my Son; today I have become your Father." God is affirming Jesus's divine mission and unique relationship with Him as His Son.

This moment connects to Moses's story, where God assured him of His presence from a burning bush, just as He now sends the Spirit to accompany Jesus (Exodus 3:12). Just like Moses, who led people from physical bondage, Jesus will lead humanity from the bondage of sin to the freedom of salvation.

Jesus's baptism reveals His identity as Messiah and offers a glimpse of the Trinity—Father, Son, and Holy Spirit—in perfect unity. This united presence affirms God's purpose and love, a partnership that will continue through Jesus's ministry.

For believers, Jesus's baptism reminds us of the significance of our own baptism, marking our spiritual union with Christ. It reassures us that, as baptized believers, we're adopted as God's children, heirs to His promise. Paul reflects this in Galatians 3:26-29, saying that all who are baptized into Christ are united as God's family, transcending all barriers.

As we reflect on Jesus's baptism, we're encouraged to think about our own faith journey. Just as Jesus received His Father's affirmation, we can begin our walk with Christ, secure in the knowledge that we, too, are loved and chosen by God. This event continues to inspire believers, reminding us of the unity, love, and purpose that shape our calling as followers of Jesus.

Journal Questions

1. **Identifying with Humanity:** Jesus chose to be baptized, even though He was without sin, to fully identify with us. What are the ways in your life where you have chosen to stand alongside others, even if it requires humility? How might this inspire you to connect with others on a deeper level?
2. **Obedience and Trust:** John initially resisted baptizing Jesus, yet ultimately obeyed when Jesus reassured him. Have you ever felt hesitant to follow God's direction? How did you move past it, and what helped you trust in God's plan?
3. **Understanding Baptism's Significance:** Jesus's baptism marked the beginning of His public ministry and showed His commitment to God's plan. If you are baptized, how do you view this commitment in your own life? What significance does your baptism hold for you today?
4. **Hearing God's Affirmation:** When God spoke from heaven, He affirmed Jesus's identity and mission. Reflecting on this moment, do you feel affirmed in your identity as a child of God? In

what ways can you remind yourself of God's love and purpose for you?
5. **Living as a Witness of Peace and Unity:** The Holy Spirit descended on Jesus in the form of a dove, symbolizing peace, and the start of a new covenant. How can you be a source of peace in your relationships and community? How does knowing you have the Holy Spirit's guidance shape your actions and decisions as a follower of Christ?

2

Mark 3:16

The time had come for Jesus to select and appoint His apostles. Until this point, many people had been following Him for different reasons; some were seeking healing, others wanted to learn from Him, and some followed because He had called them personally. In Mark's Gospel, we see that Jesus had already chosen several of the twelve, and now it was time to complete this specially appointed group.

The Gospel of Luke gives us more insight into what happened before Jesus made His choices. Luke 6:12 tells us that Jesus "went out to a mountainside to pray and spent the night praying to God." This wasn't a one-time thing; it was something Jesus did regularly throughout His ministry. Choosing the twelve apostles wasn't a random act. It was a decision made after long prayer and communion with God.

At this time, Jesus had many disciples—students who traveled with Him and learned from His teaching. Now, He was ready to choose twelve who would be called "apostles," meaning "messengers." These twelve, having been taught by Jesus, would be sent out to spread the good news to Israel. The reasons He chose these specific twelve remain mysterious. We know little about most of them, and none seemed especially skilled at preaching. Yet, they were chosen to be His special messengers, sent to teach, preach, and perform miracles in Jesus' name.

Mark lists the twelve, beginning with "Simon (to whom He gave the name Peter)." Jesus gave Simon the name Peter, meaning "rock." Matthew's Gospel records Jesus telling Peter, "And I tell you that you are Peter, and on this rock I will build my church" (Matthew 16:18). Following Peter were James and John, the sons of Zebedee, whom Jesus called "Boanerges," meaning "Sons of Thunder." We know a little about some of the others: Matthew was a tax collector, Thomas was also called "Didymus," meaning "twin," and Judas was the one who would later betray Jesus. Including Judas in the twelve reminds us that being chosen by God doesn't guarantee we'll make righteous choices. Paul touches on this in Ephesians, where he writes, "He chose us in Him before the foundation of the world, that we should be holy and blameless before Him" (Ephesians 1:4). God chooses all of us to be His children, but we must make the commitment to follow Him.

Jesus chose men from various backgrounds, showing how inclusive His Kingdom is. This diversity highlights how Christ's call can transform lives. Paul explains in 1 Corinthians 1:26-29 that God often chooses the weak and ordinary to show His power and wisdom. Jesus transformed fishermen into fishers of men and a tax collector into a messenger of God's love.

Choosing the apostles shows God's power to select people for His divine purposes. God continues to call believers today for special roles in His Kingdom (Ephesians 2:10). This shows how God is involved in shaping history and fulfilling His plans (Romans 8:28). The diversity within the church today reflects the beauty of unity in Christ, where every believer has a unique role in advancing God's Kingdom.

The story of Gideon in the Old Testament is similar. God called Gideon to lead Israel against the Midianites. At first, Gideon doubted his ability, saying he was from the weakest clan in Manasseh and was the least in his family (Judges 6:15). But God assured him, saying, "I will be with you" (Judges 6:16). Despite his doubts, Gideon followed God's call and, with only 300 men, defeated the Midianites. This story, like the calling of the apostles, shows that God often chooses unlikely people for great tasks, displaying His power instead of human strength.

Each believer has unique gifts given by the Holy Spirit. Paul discusses these spiritual gifts in Romans 12:3-8 and 1 Corinthians 12, explaining that every Christian is given gifts. Scripture doesn't specify if these gifts are given at birth or rebirth, but Paul assures us that they are from God. As Christians, it's our responsibility to seek out our spiritual gifts, listen to the Holy Spirit, and use them in our lives and ministry.

These gifts become part of our spiritual identity, helping us to grow closer to Jesus. Just as Jesus has given us these gifts, we are called to use them to serve others in His name. Paul writes, "If anyone is in Christ, the new creation has come: The old has gone, the new is here!" (2 Corinthians 5:17). We aren't perfect, but we grow into the roles Jesus has for us with the help of the Holy Spirit.

Jesus took the initiative in calling the people He wanted. They came from the crowd. He chose twelve men to help Him, and these twelve would teach others, leading to the growth of more disciples. This was how Jesus planned to spread His Church to the ends of the earth.

Journal Questions

1. **Choosing with Purpose:** Jesus prayed all night before choosing His apostles, showing the importance of seeking God's guidance. Have you ever faced a decision that required deep prayer and reflection? How can you follow Jesus' example of seeking God's direction in your choices?
2. **Diversity in Calling:** Jesus chose a diverse group of people with various backgrounds and skills. What unique gifts or abilities do you feel God has given you? How might God use these differences in the body of Christ to fulfill His purpose?
3. **Answering God's Call Despite Doubts:** Like Gideon in the Old Testament, some apostles may have felt unqualified for

their calling. Have you ever felt unsure of your abilities to fulfill what God asks of you? How can you find strength and confidence in God's promise to be with you, even when you feel weak?

4. **Embracing New Identity:** Jesus gave Simon a new name, Peter, marking his new role in God's plan. In what ways has your faith journey shaped your identity? Are there qualities or "new names" God is calling you to embrace in your life?

5. **Serving in Unity and Purpose:** Jesus chose twelve apostles to help carry His message to the world. How do you see yourself as part of this ongoing mission to share God's love? How can you use your spiritual gifts to serve and support others in your community?

3

Luke 3:16

Imagine the scene in Luke 3:16. Jesus is approaching His cousin, John the Baptist, who stands in the Jordan River, calling people to turn from their sins. Jesus, ready to begin His mission, will be baptized by John, marking the start of His journey to the cross. Luke sets up this moment with a look back to the prophets of the Old Testament, like Jeremiah, Hosea, and Micah, who often began their messages by telling their audience about the times they lived in. In Jeremiah 1:2-3, for example, the historical details set up his warning of God's judgment. Similarly, Hosea 1:1 and Micah 1:1 give context for their messages, warning Israel and Judah of the trouble they'd face due to their sins. John's calling, though many years later, shares a similar message: turn back to God before it's too late.

After setting the scene in Luke 3:1-2, Luke links John's role to the prophecy in Isaiah 40:3-5, describing John as "a voice of one calling in the wilderness." People flocked to John, not just to hear him but to see if he might be the promised Messiah. But John's mission was to prepare the way for Jesus, not to claim that role for himself. When people asked John what they should do, he told them to live rightly and treat others with kindness and fairness, pointing to Jesus' future teaching in Luke 6:31, "Do to others as you would have them do to you."

When John speaks about the coming baptism of the Holy Spirit, he points ahead to Pentecost (Acts 2), when the Spirit will empower

Jesus' followers to spread His message to the world. John's baptism with water prepared people's hearts, but he made it clear that Jesus would bring something even greater. At Pentecost, Peter explains that this moment fulfills the prophecy in Joel 2:28-32, where God promises to pour out His Spirit on everyone. From Joel's prophecy to John's preaching to the work of the Holy Spirit, we see God's plan for inner transformation. This change happens through the Spirit, who helps us overcome sin and grow closer to God.

Paul explains in Galatians 5:22-23 what a life led by the Spirit looks like. This transformation is not instant, but over time, as we listen to the Spirit, we grow to be more like Jesus. Paul describes this process in 2 Corinthians 3:18, saying that as we focus on God's glory, we are changed into His likeness.

John's humility is clear in how he accepts his role. He knew he wasn't the Messiah and was open about it, saying he wasn't even worthy to untie Jesus' sandals (Luke 3:16). This attitude reminds us to approach our calling with humility. Just as John was bold and confident in God's work without seeking personal recognition, we, too, can trust God's purpose for our lives.

In the Old Testament, Elijah's story in 1 Kings 18:36-39 also shows someone bold in God's calling. Elijah prayed for God to send fire from heaven, and God answered, showing His power. Just as Elijah boldly called people to turn back to God, John's mission was to prepare people's hearts for Jesus. Jesus even confirms in Matthew 11:14 that John fulfills the prophecy that Elijah would return before the Messiah.

Luke 3:16 gives us valuable lessons for following Jesus. First, we see how the Holy Spirit changes us. When we live by the Spirit, we reflect Jesus' love and strength (Acts 1:8). John's mention of "fire" symbolizes how the Spirit cleanses us, helping us turn away from sin (1 Corinthians 6:11).

Second, Luke 3:16 challenges us to share Jesus with others. As we live out the Spirit's work in us, the world sees Jesus alive in our lives through our love, kindness, peace, and patience.

Finally, this verse reminds us that we are never alone. The Holy Spirit is always with us, guiding and empowering us. Luke 3:16 encourages us to trust in the Spirit's strength as we live out our faith and fulfill Jesus' command to make disciples. Knowing the Spirit is always with us gives us courage and peace.

Journal Questions

1. **Preparing the Way Like John:** John's role was to prepare people's hearts for Jesus. In what ways can you help prepare others to experience Jesus today? Are there specific actions, words, or attitudes that might help you share His message with those around you?
2. **Living by the Spirit's Power:** Luke 3:16 emphasizes the transformative work of the Holy Spirit. Are there areas in your life where you feel the need for the Spirit's guidance or strength? How can you invite the Spirit to help you grow more into the image of Christ?
3. **Humility in Service:** John understood his role and served humbly, knowing he wasn't the Messiah. How does John's humility inspire you in your own service to others? Are there ways you can serve God more humbly in your daily life?
4. **Transformation Over Time:** Paul explains that the Spirit helps believers grow and change over time. Can you recall moments in your life where you've noticed this transformation? What "fruits of the Spirit" do you hope to see more of as you continue walking with God?
5. **Trusting God's Presence:** Knowing the Holy Spirit is always with us can give us courage. Are there situations where you find it hard to trust in the Spirit's guidance or presence? How might you remind yourself of His constant presence and support in those moments?

John 3:16

John 3:16 is one of the Bible's most recognized and powerful verse, showing just how deep God's love is for everyone. This verse explains that God loves us so much that He sent His only Son to save us. Like a bright light in darkness, He draws us closer to God, reminding us of His plan to save humanity. Through Jesus, God offers eternal life to anyone who believes in Him. This message of salvation appears throughout the Bible, showing us that it's a gift from God that we receive by faith. John 3:16 invites us to accept this love, live with gratitude and obedience, and share this hope with others.

This famous verse is part of a conversation between Jesus and Nicodemus, a Pharisee and a leader on the Jewish council called the Sanhedrin. They met at night, possibly for privacy since other Pharisees opposed Jesus, or simply as a convenient time. In the Bible, "night" often means more than just the time of day—it can symbolize spiritual darkness, confusion, and separation from God. In John 9:4-5, Jesus says, "While I am in the world, I am the light of the world." This shows that walking with Jesus means living in the light, free from the darkness that leads to sin.

The main lesson Jesus shares with Nicodemus is that everyone needs to place their faith in Him. Nicodemus was curious about the miracles Jesus performed, but Jesus explained that Nicodemus needed a "new birth" to truly understand God's Kingdom. While Nicodemus thought Jesus meant a literal rebirth, Jesus was actually speaking of a spiritual rebirth. This idea is also echoed in Titus 3:5, which says, "He saved us...through the washing of rebirth and renewal by the Holy Spirit." This "new birth" happens when we put our faith in Jesus.

"For God so loved the world" shows why God sent His Son. His love is for everyone on Earth, and no one is beyond His reach. God's love led Him to take action—He didn't wait for us to earn His favor; He gave it freely. Romans 5:8 says, "While we were still sinners, Christ died for us," showing that God's love is unconditional and offered to all, no matter their past.

"He gave His one and only Son" represents the greatest gift God could give. Jesus shows us what love in action truly looks like. 1 John 4:9 says, "This is how God showed his love among us: He sent his one and only Son into the world that we might live through him." God's love doesn't depend on us loving Him first—it's shown through Jesus' sacrifice for us.

"That whoever believes in Him" is an invitation for everyone. This belief isn't just agreeing with Jesus' teachings; it's putting complete faith in Him. Romans 10:9 says, "If you declare with your mouth, 'Jesus is Lord,' and believe in your heart that God raised him from the dead, you will be saved." This belief is the start of a lifelong journey of following Jesus and growing to be more like Him in what we think, say, and do.

"Shall not perish but have eternal life" is a promise that only Jesus can make. Here, "perishing" is more than physical death—it's being separated from God forever. Eternal life, on the other hand, means living with God forever through faith in Jesus. Romans 6:23 puts it this way: "For the wages of sin is death, but the gift of God is eternal life in Christ Jesus our Lord." Sin leads to death, but eternal life is God's free gift to those who believe and follow Jesus.

Nicodemus' journey from curiosity to faith reflects the message of John 3:16. He sought out Jesus, intrigued by His teachings and miracles. Though he was a respected leader, he came to Jesus with questions, sensing something special about Him. In John 3:1-21, Jesus explains to Nicodemus about being "born again" and reveals God's love for the world—that God sent His only Son so that anyone who believes in Him can have eternal life.

At first, Nicodemus was confused, but Jesus' words planted a seed of faith. Later, Nicodemus defends Jesus before the Pharisees (John 7:50-52) and helps prepare His body for burial after the crucifixion (John 19:39-40), showing his belief and devotion. Nicodemus' journey mirrors the message of Isaiah 45:22, where God says, "Turn to me and be saved, all you ends of the earth." God's love and salvation are for everyone, including Nicodemus.

John 3:16 shows God's love and His plan for our salvation. His love is limitless, available to everyone, and is a gift we can't earn. Ephesians 2:8-9 reminds us that we're saved by faith, not by our own works. Romans 15:13 encourages us to trust in God so we can be filled with joy, peace, and hope through the Holy Spirit. John 3:16 is Jesus' invitation to us, offering salvation, eternal life, and a new way of living—one that we're called to accept.

Journal Questions

1. **Understanding God's Love:** John 3:16 reveals God's immense love for the world. How does this understanding of God's love shape the way you view yourself and others? Are there ways you can reflect this love in your interactions with people daily?
2. **Embracing Spiritual Rebirth:** Jesus tells Nicodemus that he must be "born again" to see the Kingdom of God. What does it mean for you to be spiritually reborn, and how has your life changed since accepting Jesus? Are there areas in your life where you still seek God's renewal?
3. **Living in the Light:** John's Gospel often contrasts light with darkness, showing that those who follow Jesus walk in the light. Are there areas of "darkness" (like fears, habits, or thoughts) where you need God's light? How can walking with Jesus help you overcome these challenges?

4. **Believing as a Lifelong Journey:** Faith in Jesus is described as a journey, not just a one-time decision. How has your belief in Jesus grown or changed over time? What practices or habits could help you strengthen and deepen your faith daily?
5. **Trusting in Eternal Life:** John 3:16 promises eternal life to all who believe in Jesus. How does this promise give you hope for the future? How can focusing on God's eternal promises help you handle difficulties or setbacks in life?

5

Acts 3:16

The book of Acts tells the story of the early church leaders who spread the message of the Gospel by preaching, teaching, and healing the sick, guided by the Holy Spirit. In Acts Chapter 3, we read about an amazing event involving Peter, John, and a crippled man.

As Peter and John were heading to the temple for the evening prayer, they encountered this man at a gate called "Beautiful," where many devout Jews were entering. It was common in those days to see beggars at places with heavy foot traffic, such as the temple entrance, similar to how we might see homeless individuals on busy streets today. As Peter and John passed by, they noticed the crippled man, who had been there many times before. People likely recognized him since he had been crippled from birth, as we learn in verse 2. While many walked past him without a second glance, perhaps having given him money before or simply choosing to ignore him, Peter and John did not. The man hoped for some money or food as he looked around for help, but Peter and John gave him something far more valuable.

In verse 4, it says, "Peter looked straight at him, as did John." This man was expecting them to offer him money, but what he received was beyond his wildest dreams—a solution to his lifelong struggle. Peter told him, "Silver or gold I do not have, but what I do have I give you. In the name of Jesus Christ of Nazareth, walk" (Acts 3:6). This teaches us an important lesson: even when we don't have material things to give, we can still offer something valuable to those in need.

God used this man's physical disability as an opportunity to show His power through Peter and John. They did not heal the man by their own strength but through faith in Jesus' name. Peter explained to the crowd, "By faith in the name of Jesus, this man whom you see and know was made strong. It is Jesus' name and the faith that comes through him that has completely healed him" (Acts 3:16).

The healing of this man is a powerful example of what can happen when we act in faith. Peter and John knew that the man could be healed by Jesus' power, and the crippled man, in turn, responded with faith in a way he never had before. Like the crippled man, all of us face challenges that test our faith, and sometimes, only God's intervention can bring us through.

This story in Acts shows us that God can turn adversity into an opportunity for transformation. The crippled man's healing gave him freedom from a lifetime of suffering. Before this, he couldn't walk or take care of himself, and because of his disability, he wasn't even allowed to enter the temple for spiritual care. This healing not only freed him physically but also allowed him to join in the spiritual life of the community. God's name, Jehovah Rapha, means "the Lord who heals" (Psalm 103:3), and this healing was a clear sign of God's compassion and power.

When the man was healed, he entered the temple with Peter and John, walking and jumping with joy. His excitement drew a crowd, and Peter used this opportunity to preach about repentance, just as he did in Acts Chapter 2. The miracle of the healing was a chance for Peter to call the people to choose between God's blessing or the curse of exclusion. God's mercy was extended to all through this moment of healing.

This event also fulfilled prophecies from the Old Testament, like in Isaiah 35:6, which says, "Then will the lame leap like a deer," a clear connection to the man jumping for joy. Isaiah also spoke of God's compassion in Isaiah 61:1, where God promises to free people from oppression. Just as Peter, empowered by the Holy Spirit, freed the crippled man from his disability, we see the fulfillment of God's promises.

The significance of faith in this healing reminds us of another story from the Gospels—the story of the Roman centurion. In this account, a centurion approached Jesus to ask for his servant to be healed. Even though the centurion was not Jewish, he believed that Jesus had the authority to heal his servant from afar. He said to Jesus, "Just say the word, and my servant will be healed" (Matthew 8:8). This great faith astonished Jesus, and the servant was healed at that very moment. The centurion's faith is similar to the faith demonstrated in Acts 3, where the healing came not from Peter's power, but through faith in the name of Jesus.

In Acts 3:16, Peter explains to the crowd that it was "faith in the name of Jesus" that healed the crippled man. The miracle wasn't about Peter or John's abilities—it was about the power of Jesus' name and faith in Him. This teaches us how important faith is in our own lives, not only for physical healing but for spiritual renewal and restoration.

Peter's explanation also points to the authority that Jesus has over everything, just like the centurion recognized. In the Bible, someone's "name" is more than just a label—it represents their character, power, and essence. Philippians 2:9-11 tells us that Jesus' name is "above every name," and that "at the name of Jesus every knee should bow." The power of Jesus' name is a reminder of His authority and His ability to heal, transform, and restore our lives.

This story in Acts Chapter 3 teaches us that faith in Jesus can lead to incredible changes, both in our own lives and in the lives of others. Just as Peter and John healed the crippled man, we too can be agents of God's healing and restoration through faith, prayer, and the power of the Holy Spirit. The healing of the crippled man is not just a story of physical restoration but a message of the spiritual healing that Jesus offers to all who believe in Him.

Journal Questions

1. **Exploring Personal Transformation:** In Acts 3:16, the crippled man experiences a life-changing miracle through faith in the name of Jesus. Reflect on a moment in your life when you experienced personal growth or transformation through faith. How did this change impact your outlook on life and your relationship with God?
2. **Understanding Acts of Faith:** Peter and John acted with great faith, believing in the power of Jesus' name to heal the crippled man. Think about a time when you stepped out in faith, trusting God for something that seemed impossible. How did your faith influence the outcome, and what did you learn from the experience?
3. **Responding to God's Healing Power:** The crippled man went from being unable to walk to leaping for joy, demonstrating the power of God's healing. Reflect on a time when you or someone you know experienced God's healing, whether physically, emotionally, or spiritually. How did this healing change your view of God's presence in your life?
4. **Embracing the Role of the Holy Spirit:** Peter and John were able to heal the crippled man through the power of the Holy Spirit. How have you experienced the Holy Spirit's guidance or empowerment in your own life? How did the Holy Spirit help you face challenges or serve others in ways you couldn't have done on your own?
5. **Understanding the Power of Jesus' Name:** Acts 3:16 emphasizes that the healing was done through "faith in the name of Jesus." How does understanding the power and authority of Jesus' name influence the way you pray, live, or approach challenges in your life? What does it mean for you personally to trust in the power of Jesus' name?

6

Romans 3:16

Romans 3:16 is one of the shortest verses we will study, and it is also one of the darkest. The verse says, "ruin and misery mark their ways," which might make you wonder why we're focusing on such a negative message. However, it's important to read the verses around it for a better understanding. By doing this, we can see how this verse fits into the larger message Paul is delivering in his letter to the churches in Rome. So, let's take a closer look at Romans 3:16 and the context around it.

Romans 3:16 is part of Paul's argument about the universal condition of humanity. He explains that both Jews and Gentiles are guilty of sin and are in need of God's grace. In Romans 1, Paul describes how the Gentiles turned away from God by worshipping idols and committing various sins. In Romans 2, Paul addresses the Jews, telling them they are also guilty because, even though they had the Law, they still chose to live sinfully. By Romans 3, Paul makes it clear that no one is exempt from their sins.

Paul's description of humanity during his time mirrors the violence and corruption we see in Genesis 6:11-12 during Noah's time, when God saw that the whole earth was corrupt. In Romans, Paul is addressing the sinful state of humanity and urging people to seek God. He uses quotes from the Psalms, Ecclesiastes, and Isaiah to show how deep this sinfulness goes. Romans 3:16 paints a vivid picture of where sin leads—ruin and misery.

A key point Paul makes is that God isn't just concerned with outward actions, like circumcision, but with the condition of the heart. In Romans 2:26, Paul says, "So then, if those who are not circumcised keep the law's requirements, will they not be regarded as though they were circumcised?" This means God values an inward life of faithfulness over mere outward expressions of faith.

Paul continues to emphasize the brokenness of humanity by stating in Romans 3:23, "all have sinned and fall short of the glory of God." He wants readers to understand that we are all guilty and in need of salvation. The point Paul is driving home is that no one can claim righteousness based on their own efforts. Instead, we all must look to Jesus for redemption.

Although Paul's description of sin in Romans 3 is bleak, he is leading us to the ultimate truth of God's love. Romans 5:8 tells us, "But God demonstrates his own love for us in this: While we were still sinners, Christ died for us." Even though sin leads to ruin and misery, God offers a way out through the sacrifice of Jesus. Salvation is not just about escaping punishment but about being restored to a life of purpose and wholeness through Jesus.

The Bible shows us over and over that God's plan is not one of condemnation but one of renewal and salvation. In 2 Corinthians 5:17, we are reminded, "Therefore, if anyone is in Christ, the new creation has come: The old has gone, the new is here!" This new life begins when we place our faith in Jesus. He takes away the old patterns of sin and replaces them with a renewed life in Him.

Romans 3:16 describes the path of destruction that comes from rejecting God, and a biblical example of this is King Saul. Saul started out as the first king of Israel with great promise, but he disobeyed God and allowed jealousy and sin to take over his life. His downfall began in 1 Samuel 15, when he disobeyed God's command to destroy everything belonging to the Amalekites. His failure to obey cost him the kingdom. Saul's jealousy of David further fueled his ruin, leading him down a path of paranoia and anger, which ended in his tragic death (1 Samuel 31).

King Saul's story is a powerful example of the truth in Romans 3:16. His disobedience brought ruin and misery not just to himself but to his family and the nation of Israel. Saul's failure to repent fully from his ways led to his downfall, showing how sin and rejection of God's Will can have devastating consequences.

Yet, even in the midst of this tragic story, Romans 3:16 also points us to the hope of grace. While Saul's actions remind us of the severity of sin, we are called to extend the same grace that God has shown us. In Matthew 18:21-22, when Peter asks Jesus how many times we should forgive, Jesus replies, "seventy-seven times." Just as God has forgiven us, we must show forgiveness and grace to others. It's not just about believing in God's grace for us; it's about living it out in our relationships and actions.

Romans 3:16 is a part of Paul's larger message about the brokenness of humanity and the consequences of sin. But it also points us to the hope and redemption found in God's love through Jesus Christ. While sin brings ruin and misery, God's gift of salvation offers renewal and restoration. We are called to accept that grace, live faithfully, and reflect God's love to others.

Journal Questions

1. **Recognizing the Consequences of Sin:** Romans 3:16 speaks of the ruin and misery that come from rejecting God's will. Reflect on a time in your life when you experienced the consequences of sin or disobedience. How did this experience deepen your understanding of the impact of sin and the need for God's grace?
2. **Embracing Grace After Failure:** King Saul's downfall was marked by his refusal to fully repent. Can you recall a moment in your life when you struggled with repentance or accepting God's grace after failure? How did you eventually come to embrace His forgiveness, and how did it transform your heart?

3. **Seeking Inner Transformation Over Outward Actions:** Paul emphasizes that God values the condition of the heart over outward religious expressions. Reflect on a time when you realized that your faith needed to go beyond rituals or traditions. How did this shift affect your relationship with God and your spiritual growth?
4. **Living Out God's Grace in Relationships:** Matthew 18:21-22 challenges us to forgive others just as we've been forgiven. Think of a time when you had to extend grace to someone who wronged you. How did practicing forgiveness in this situation change your perspective on God's grace in your own life?
5. **Finding Hope in God's Love Amid Brokenness:** Despite the bleak description of humanity's sinfulness in Romans 3, Paul leads us to the hope found in Jesus. Reflect on a time when you were overwhelmed by personal struggles or brokenness. How did the message of God's love and the promise of renewal through Jesus give you hope during that season?

7

1 Corinthians 3:16

1 Corinthians 3:16, comes from a letter Paul is writing to the church he had established in Corinth. He finds the church struggling to live as true followers of Jesus Christ. Even though, through Paul's ministry, they had been saved from their sins, cleansed by the blood of Christ, and received the Holy Spirit, they were still behaving in ways that Paul described as "worldly." Earlier in the letter, Paul had contrasted the "spiritual person" with a non-believer, pointing out the difference between someone who follows Christ and someone who does not.

Today's church might view the Corinthians as being justified, meaning they were saved—but not sanctified. While they had faith in Jesus and identified as Christians, they had not grown in their spiritual maturity or in their relationship with God. Sanctification is the process of growing spiritually and walking closely with God, as Paul refers to in 1 Corinthians 2:16, where he talks about having "the mind of the Lord." The Corinthians struggled with the temptation of conforming to the culture around them, something that remains a challenge for Christians today.

The Corinthians were stuck in an in-between place, where they were justified but not pursuing sanctification. They were Christians, yet they still acted like non-Christians, living in worldly ways, and holding onto unconfessed sin. Paul's teaching in 1 Corinthians 3 uses three distinct images to describe their situation.

First, Paul compares the Corinthians to plants that were planted by him and Apollos. Instead of growing spiritually, they allowed division to creep in, choosing to follow either Paul or Apollos rather than focusing on their unity in Christ. This division revealed their spiritual immaturity. This kind of division is still seen in churches today, where people sometimes focus more on following a particular leader rather than following Jesus.

Next, Paul uses the image of a building, representing both individuals and the church. He explains that the building can be constructed with valuable materials like "gold, silver, and costly stones," which will survive God's testing by fire and be rewarded. Alternatively, it can be built with "wood, hay, and straw," which will be burned up, though the person may still be saved. However, Paul warns that those who destroy God's building, the church, will face severe consequences, as 1 Corinthians 3:16 identifies the church as God's temple, and those who defile it will be destroyed. This shows how highly God values the local church and its ministry.

The idea of the temple as a sacred space is deeply rooted in the Old Testament. The temple in Jerusalem was considered the physical dwelling place of God's glory, as described in 1 Kings 8:10-11, where the "glory of the Lord filled the house of the Lord." Yet, Isaiah 66:1 points to a shift from a physical temple to a broader understanding of God's dwelling among His people, where God declares, "Heaven is my throne, and the earth is my footstool. Where is the house you will build for me?"

In 1 Corinthians 3:16, Paul isn't referring to an individual's body as a temple (as he does later in 1 Corinthians 6:19), but rather to the corporate church. The Corinthians were struggling to build and maintain this spiritual temple. Paul also refers to this idea of a corporate temple in Ephesians 2:21 and 2 Corinthians 6:16. Jesus himself critiques the misuse of the physical temple in Matthew 23:38, predicting its destruction and lamenting over Jerusalem, which had rejected God and left its house desolate. This same warning applies to the Corinthians, as Paul cautions them about how they treat the church.

The imagery in 1 Corinthians 3:16 reveals that the corporate church is God's dwelling place, but it also encourages believers to see themselves as temples embodying the Holy Spirit. God's presence is not confined to a physical building but resides in the lives of believers. As Christians, we are called to live as sacred temples, set apart for God's purposes, as outlined in Leviticus 20:26, where God says, "Be holy, because I, the Lord, am holy." This calling comes with expectations of humility, holiness, forgiveness, and a commitment to build one another up in faith.

Daniel is a prime example of someone who lived out the principles of 1 Corinthians 3:16, acting as a temple of God through his holiness, discipline, and faith. Despite living in Babylon, a land full of temptation, Daniel refused to defile himself with the king's food and wine (Daniel 1:8), choosing to remain set apart for God. This reflects the idea in 1 Corinthians 3:16 that believers are God's temples and must honor God with their lives.

Daniel's spiritual discipline is further demonstrated by his commitment to prayer, even when it was forbidden by law. Daniel 6:10 recounts how he continued praying three times a day, despite the threat of being thrown into the lions' den. His faithfulness shows the deep connection between the believer and God, modeling how one should live as a temple of the Holy Spirit.

When Daniel was thrown into the lions' den, he refused to conform to Babylonian culture and remained faithful to God. His deliverance from the lions reflects Romans 12:2 and its call for believers not to conform to the world but to live according to God's will. Daniel's life serves as a testimony to God's power, much like how believers today are called to reflect God's presence through their actions.

Just as God's presence filled the temple in the Old Testament, now His Spirit dwells in believers through Christ. 1 Corinthians 6:19 says, "Do you not know that your bodies are temples of the Holy Spirit, who is in you, whom you have received from God?" Jesus is the cornerstone of this new temple, as seen in Matthew 21:42, where He says, "The stone the builders rejected has become the cornerstone." Without Jesus as our foundation, we risk falling into worldly behavior, just as the Corinthians did. We must rely on Christ, the cornerstone, because our eternal future depends on it.

Journal Questions

1. **Exploring Holiness and Identity:** In 1 Corinthians 3:16, Paul teaches that believers are temples of the Holy Spirit, set apart for God's purposes. Reflect on a time when you became more aware of your identity as a dwelling place for God's Spirit. How did this understanding affect the way you live, make decisions, or view yourself in relation to God?
2. **Embracing Spiritual Discipline:** Daniel, in his commitment to prayer and holiness, embodied what it means to live as a temple of God. Think about a time when spiritual discipline, such as prayer or studying Scripture, brought about growth or change in your life. How did these practices shape your relationship with God and help you resist worldly temptations?
3. **Facing Cultural Pressures with Faith:** Daniel refused to conform to Babylonian culture, even when it threatened his life. Have you ever faced pressure to conform to the world's values or ways of living? How did your faith help you stand firm, and what lessons did you learn about living as a temple of the Holy Spirit in a secular world?
4. **Experiencing the Power of God's Presence:** Paul warns that the church is God's temple, and those who harm it will face consequences. Reflect on a time when you experienced the power of God's presence within a community of believers. How did this experience deepen your understanding of being part of the corporate body of Christ, and how did it inspire you to contribute to the health and unity of the church?
5. **Trusting Jesus as the Cornerstone:** In Matthew 21:42, Jesus is described as the cornerstone of our faith. Think of a time when trusting in Jesus as your foundation helped you through a diffi-

cult situation or challenge. How did this reliance on Christ reshape your perspective and strengthen your faith during that time?

8

2 Corinthians 3:16

"Unveiled Glory" could very well be a title of this chapter because Paul, in this chapter, references the event in Exodus 34:29-35 to give readers a clear example of the difference between the old covenant given to Moses and the new covenant brought by Jesus. This contrast also supports Paul's qualifications as an apostle, since his authority, likely being questioned by others, is not established by credentials written on stone tablets, as was the old Law. Instead, Paul's ministry is written on the hearts of believers by the Spirit of the living God.

Paul starts by contrasting the old covenant, represented by the Mosaic Law, with the new covenant, which is empowered by the Holy Spirit. The old covenant was "written in letters on stone" (2 Corinthians 3:7), referring to the Ten Commandments and the laws that governed Israel. Though the laws that came after the Ten Commandments were important, they were rigid and could not produce lasting change in the hearts of people. They revealed sin but could not provide the power to overcome it, leading Paul to describe the old covenant as a "ministry that brought death."

In contrast, the new covenant is centered on the Spirit, which brings life and transformation to the believer's heart. Paul writes that the new covenant "gives life," and believers are "ministers of a new covenant—not of the letter but of the Spirit" (2 Corinthians 3:6). What Paul emphasizes is not just how the new covenant was established but that its ministry operates through the Spirit, not through the letter of the law.

Even though the old covenant had its own glory—such as when Moses' face glowed after being in the presence of God—it pales in comparison to the new covenant brought by Christ. The Old Testament Law was good, righteous, and holy, given to Moses through a miraculous series of events. Yet, Paul explains in 2 Corinthians 3:9 that while the old covenant brought condemnation, the new covenant brings righteousness. He questions, "How much more glorious will the ministry that brings righteousness be compared to the ministry that brought condemnation?"

Moses' glowing face after receiving the Law from God on Mount Sinai scared the Hebrews, including his brother Aaron. Because of this, Moses wore a veil over his face whenever he wasn't in the presence of God. The unveiling of his face symbolized receiving revelation and truth directly from God. However, the veil also became an obstacle for the Hebrews, preventing them from fully understanding God's will. Paul uses this imagery to explain how the Jewish people have metaphorically placed a veil over their hearts, preventing them from experiencing the glory and freedom of the new covenant through Jesus Christ.

Paul describes the powerful transformation that occurs when individuals turn to Christ. "But whenever anyone turns to the Lord, the veil is taken away" (2 Corinthians 3:16). The lifting of this veil is a metaphor for the removal of spiritual blindness, allowing believers to see the truth of God's presence and His redemptive work through Jesus. The law, as Paul mentions in Romans 7:6, was holy but could not bring life. While it revealed sin, it did not provide a path to overcoming it. Through the Holy Spirit, however, believers are given a new heart and mind, enabling them to live fully in God's truth.

Paul emphasizes the crucial role of the Holy Spirit in the process of unveiling. It is the Spirit who enables believers to understand the mysteries of God's kingdom and to walk in the light of His truth. Jesus affirmed this in John 16:13, saying, "But when He, the Spirit of truth, comes, He will guide you into all the truth." The ongoing work of the Holy Spirit is what transforms believers, allowing them to experience deeper intimacy with God and greater understanding of their identity as God's children and heirs to His kingdom.

An excellent example of this transformation is seen in the life of King Josiah. Josiah became king of Judah at a young age, inheriting a kingdom steeped in idolatry and sin. The nation had turned away from God, worshiping false gods and neglecting the Law. But when Josiah was in his twenties, he sought to restore the true worship of God. During the renovation of the temple, the Book of the Law was found, and upon hearing its words, Josiah tore his clothes in deep repentance, realizing how far the people had strayed from God (2 Kings 22:11).

At that moment, it was as if the "veil" of spiritual blindness had been lifted. Josiah led sweeping reforms throughout Judah, destroying idols, reinstating the Passover, and calling the people back to worship God according to His laws. His transformation—from a king presiding over a corrupt nation to a devoted servant of God—mirrors the removal of spiritual blindness described by Paul in 2 Corinthians 3:16.

The psalmist also echoes this idea in Psalm 119:18, praying, "Open my eyes that I may see wonderful things in your law." Just like Josiah, whose eyes were opened to the truth of God's Word, believers who turn to the Lord experience the removal of the veil, allowing them to see and understand God's truth.

2 Corinthians 3:16 offers practical applications for believers today. It illustrates the powerful transformation that happens when someone turns to Christ and the veil of spiritual blindness is lifted. This veil, like the one Moses wore, represents the barriers between humanity and God. But through faith in Christ, believers gain direct access to God's presence and His transformative grace.

Paul also reminds believers that they are temples of the Holy Spirit (1 Corinthians 6:19), which means they are called to live lives that reflect this reality. The lifting of the veil signifies not only the removal of spiritual ignorance but also the beginning of a new life in which the Holy Spirit actively transforms the believer's heart.

Paul taught that a figurative veil of spiritual blindness had covered the minds and hearts of most Jewish people. In Christ, the masks and veils people wear to hide their weaknesses and insecurities can be permanently removed. The sooner believers allow these veils to be taken off, the better, because they obscure their view of Christ in His full glory. Removing the veil also enables believers to reflect Christ's glory to others, as Paul explains in 2 Corinthians 3:18, where he speaks of being transformed "from glory to glory" through the work of the Holy Spirit.

Journal Questions

1. **Exploring the Veil Imagery:** How does Paul use the story of Moses and the veil in Exodus 34:29-35 to explain the difference between the old covenant and the new covenant? How does this imagery help us understand the spiritual blindness that comes from not turning to Christ?
2. **Comparing Covenants:** In 2 Corinthians 3, Paul contrasts the old covenant, which brought death, with the new covenant, which brings life through the Spirit. What are some key differences between the old covenant and the new covenant? How do these differences impact the way we live out our faith today?
3. **The Role of the Holy Spirit:** How does Paul describe the role of the Holy Spirit in unveiling the truth and guiding believers in their relationship with God? How does the Holy Spirit continue to transform the hearts and minds of believers today?
4. **Relating to King Josiah's Transformation:** In what ways does King Josiah's story reflect the transformation that occurs when the "veil" of spiritual blindness is lifted? How does his response to discovering the Book of the Law parallel the experience of turning to Christ in faith?

5. **Personal Reflection on the Veil:** Paul explains that in Christ, the veil of spiritual blindness is removed. What "veils" might still obscure your view of Christ's glory in your life, and how can you allow the Holy Spirit to remove them to deepen your understanding and relationship with God?

9

Galatians 3:16

Galatians 3:16 is a key verse in Paul's argument to the Galatian church, explaining the difference between salvation through the works of the law and the freedom of salvation through faith in Christ. Paul, along with other writers in the New Testament, takes the firm position that salvation can only be found through faith, not by following the law. The law served its purpose, but now, Paul shifts the focus to Abraham's "seed." In Galatians 3:16, Paul emphasizes that God's promise to Abraham did not refer to many descendants (plural), but to one singular "seed"—Jesus Christ.

During this period, the Galatian church was in turmoil, with some members believing that adherence to the law was more important than Christ's sacrifice. In response, Paul takes an aggressive stance, even calling the Galatians "foolish" (Galatians 3:1) for thinking that works could achieve salvation. He draws attention to God's covenant with Abraham, explaining that God's promises in Genesis 12:7, 13:15, 15:5, and 24:7 were about one specific descendant—Christ—rather than many. Paul's use of the singular "seed" points directly to Jesus, highlighting the exclusive nature of His role in God's redemptive plan.

In Genesis 12:2-3, God's promises to Abraham consistently point toward the future, with God saying "I will" numerous times. Abraham was counted as righteous because of his faith, not by his actions, which confirms that God's promises would be fulfilled through faith.

Paul connects this promise directly to Christ, explaining that the "seed" God promised to Abraham was Jesus. This reveals the exclusivity of Christ as the fulfillment of God's promises and emphasizes His central role in the unfolding of God's redemptive plan. Paul explains that God's promise was never about a multitude of sons, but about one particular Son—Jesus—who would come at the appointed time and then bless all nations through Him.

Paul was not alone in teaching that salvation is exclusively through Christ. In John 14:6, Jesus Himself tells Thomas, "I am the way and the truth and the life. No one comes to the Father except through me." This statement reinforces that a relationship with God is possible only through faith in Christ. Humanity has been trapped in darkness due to sin, but God sent His Son into the world to bring the light of salvation and eternal life to everyone who believes in Him. Paul echoes this idea in 1 Timothy 2:5, where he writes, "For there is one God and one mediator between God and mankind, the man Christ Jesus." This verse affirms Jesus' divine authority and His unique role as the mediator who reconciles humanity with God, calling them to repentance and faith.

By linking God's promises to Abraham with faith in Christ, Paul highlights that salvation does not come through obedience to the law or human effort but through faith in the finished work of Jesus on the cross. Galatians 3:16 stresses that salvation is a gift from God, given freely and received only by faith in Christ. This grace, which Jesus embodies, cannot be earned by works but is a manifestation of God's love and mercy, accessible through belief in His Son.

Faith in Jesus enables believers to experience the love of God. Through faith, humanity connects with God on a spiritual level, leading to transformation, spiritual growth, and the development of a relationship with Him. This faith brings about a moral revival in the believer's life, raising them spiritually and leading them toward eternal life. As faith deepens, so does love for God and others, fostering an ever-growing connection with the divine.

David's life exemplifies the promise found in Galatians 3:16, as he also foreshadows the fulfillment of God's covenant through Christ. While the promise was first made to Abraham, it was reaffirmed to David. In 2 Samuel 7:12-13, God promises David that one of his descendants will build a house for God's name and that his kingdom will last forever. Initially, it was believed this prophecy was about Solomon, but it pointed to Christ, the eternal "seed" of David who would reign forever. This covenant is reaffirmed in Psalm 89:3-4, where God says, "I have made a covenant with my chosen one, I have sworn to David my servant, 'I will establish your line forever and make your throne firm through all generations.'" This promise was not limited to David's immediate descendants but anticipated the coming of Christ, who would establish an everlasting kingdom.

David's lineage became the means through which the promised "seed"—Jesus—would come, fulfilling God's plan of salvation. Galatians 3:16 serves as a powerful reminder to place our faith in Jesus, the singular "seed" who brings salvation and establishes an eternal kingdom. This verse teaches that salvation cannot be achieved through following the law, works, or self-righteousness, but is a free gift of grace from God, accessible only through faith in Jesus. Relying on this grace encourages believers to deepen their relationship with Christ, acknowledging and accepting His transformative presence in their lives. Only through this relationship can believers experience the true transformation that God's grace offers, leading to a life aligned with His will.

Journal Questions

1. **Recognizing Christ as the Fulfillment of God's Promise:** Reflect on a time when you became aware of Christ's role as the fulfillment of God's promises, as Paul describes in Galatians 3:16. How did this realization deepen your understanding of God's faithfulness and plan for salvation? How has it impacted on your personal faith journey?

2. **Letting Go of Legalism and Embracing Grace:** Think about a time in your life when you struggled with trying to earn God's favor through works or legalistic practices. How did coming to understand that salvation is a free gift of grace, as highlighted in Galatians 3:16, change the way you relate to God? How can you continue to rest in His grace rather than your own efforts?
3. **Experiencing Spiritual Transformation through Faith:** Paul emphasizes that faith, not works, lead to salvation. Can you recall a moment when your faith in Jesus brought about a significant spiritual transformation in your life? How did this experience shape your relationship with Christ and your perspective on living by faith?
4. **Trusting in God's Long-Term Plan:** Reflect on how God's covenant with Abraham, fulfilled in Christ, has been unfolding over generations. How does trusting in God's long-term plan for humanity encourage you to trust Him with the uncertainties in your own life? Write about a situation where trusting in God's timing brought peace and clarity.
5. **Reflecting on God's Grace in Your Life:** Galatians 3:16 points to the grace of God through Christ as a gift that cannot be earned. Reflect on a time when you experienced God's grace in a powerful way. How did that experience change your outlook on faith, and how can you continue to live in a way that reflects that grace to others around you?

10

Ephesians 3:16

Paul's letter to the Ephesians was written to a church community he had started, driven by his passion to bring Gentiles to Jesus. In the letter, Paul offers encouragement, instruction, and spiritual insight. In chapter 3, Paul explains that God's grace is now available to the Gentiles because the mystery of God's plan for redeeming all of creation has been revealed through His Son, Jesus. Ephesians 3:16 is part of a prayer Paul offers to the Ephesians. The prayer culminates in verses 20-21, which have become a common doxology in the Church today.

Paul begins his prayer in humble submission, kneeling before the Father, whom he acknowledges as the one who unites all humanity into a universal family. He asks God, who is gloriously abundant, to grant the readers inner strength through the power of the Holy Spirit. This inner strength mirrors Christ's presence within the hearts of those who faithfully surrender to Him. Paul describes this unity as being "rooted and established in love" (Ephesians 3:17), with Christ dwelling in believers' hearts as the source of life and unity. Although Paul starts his prayer in submission to God as King, it quickly becomes a prayer focused on the love and care of a present God, working through His Son and the power of the Spirit within.

Paul's prayer also reveals that good fatherhood comes from God alone. Though human fathers may fall short, they succeed when they imitate God, the true Father. When human fathers succeed in relating to their children, it is through their inner obedience to God the Father.

This prayer, asking God to strengthen believers through the "glorious riches" of His grace, reflects a central theme of Paul's letter: God's generosity and abundant grace toward His people. It emphasizes the vast spiritual resources available to believers and the immeasurable blessings they receive through their union with Christ. This generosity echoes God's promises throughout Scripture. In Psalm 23:1, David declares, "The Lord is my shepherd; I lack nothing." Similarly, Philippians 4:19 reminds believers that "God will meet all your needs according to the riches of His glory in Christ Jesus."

Paul's prayer also focuses on inner strength, which is essential for the transformative work of the Holy Spirit within believers. This strength empowers them to face spiritual challenges with confidence and resilience. Isaiah 40:31 reinforces this idea: "Those who hope in the Lord will renew their strength. They will soar on wings like eagles; they will run and not grow weary."

The Holy Spirit strengthens believers from within, helping them grow, progress, and bear fruit in spiritual matters. Throughout Scripture, God's Spirit is portrayed as strengthening the weak, as seen in the lives of the judges, kings, and prophets in the Old Testament, and in the apostles in the New Testament. When our inner being is filled with the Holy Spirit, our spirit, heart, and mind are strengthened—and when they are weak, everything else becomes weak too.

Many people mistakenly think that fellowship with Christ and believing in Him are the same. In reality, fellowship is the result of faith. Christ dwells in our hearts by the Spirit and through faith, and we, as the body of the Church, dwell in Him. The fruit of this indwelling is love. Being "rooted and established in love" transforms every aspect of our lives, from our identity and character to our relationships with others. Colossians 2:6-7 emphasizes that we are to continue to live in Christ, "rooted and built up in Him, strengthened in the faith... and overflowing with thankfulness."

A figure from the Bible, who exemplifies Ephesians 3:16 is Nehemiah, a man who relied on God's strength and guidance in his mission to rebuild the walls of Jerusalem. Nehemiah's story, found in the Old Testament, demonstrates the power of inner strength that comes from God's Spirit working within a believer.

When Nehemiah first learned about the broken walls of Jerusalem, he was deeply distressed, but instead of relying on his own abilities, he turned to God in prayer. Nehemiah 1:4 says, "When I heard these things, I sat down and wept. For some days I mourned and fasted and prayed before the God of heaven." This reliance on prayer and God's strength mirrors Paul's prayer in Ephesians 3:16 for believers to be strengthened in their inner being by the Holy Spirit.

Throughout his mission, Nehemiah faced intense opposition and discouragement from enemies who tried to stop the rebuilding. Yet, he continued to rely on God's strength. In Nehemiah 6:9, when his enemies attempted to intimidate him, Nehemiah prayed, "Now strengthen my hands." This plea for divine empowerment reflects the same dependence on God's Spirit that Paul encourages in Ephesians.

Nehemiah's leadership and perseverance were not products of his own strength but were sustained by his deep connection with God. His inner resilience, driven by his faith, enabled him to complete the monumental task of rebuilding Jerusalem's walls despite opposition. Nehemiah's story illustrates how believers can find inner strength through their reliance on God's Spirit, just as Paul prayed for in Ephesians 3:16.

This prayer invites believers to explore the depth of God's love, which fuels their spiritual growth and maturity. 1 John 4:16-17 reminds us, "Whoever lives in love lives in God, and God in them." Believers are encouraged to rely on God's presence and strength in their daily lives. Psalm 46:1 reminds believers, "God is our refuge and strength, an ever-present help in trouble."

Paul's prayer urges believers to engage deeply in spiritual disciplines like prayer and studying Scripture. Joshua 1:8 teaches us to meditate on God's Word day and night so we may be strong and courageous. By following Paul's example of praying for strength and unity, we too can be firmly established in our faith and grow in it. Though God's love is beyond full comprehension, it is more than sufficient for our needs. It is the goal of believers to be filled with the love of God's Spirit, enjoying His blessings and serving as faithful witnesses of His grace to the world.

Journal Questions

1. **Drawing Inner Strength from God like Nehemiah:** Nehemiah faced intense opposition while rebuilding Jerusalem's walls but relied on God's strength through prayer. Reflect on the time when you faced a difficult challenge. How did turning to God for strength, like Nehemiah, help you overcome that challenge, and how did it deepen your faith?
2. **Relying on God's Spirit in Times of Uncertainty:** Nehemiah trusted God for guidance and strength during uncertain times. Think of a time when you, too, faced uncertainty. How did your reliance on the Holy Spirit help you navigate that situation? What impact did it have on your spiritual growth?
3. **Experiencing the Holy Spirit's Empowerment:** Ephesians 3:16 speaks of being strengthened in the inner being by the Holy Spirit. Can you recall a moment when you felt empowered by the Holy Spirit during a difficult season? How did this experience transform your perspective on facing challenges?
4. **Rooted and Grounded in Love:** Paul's prayer in Ephesians 3:16 emphasizes being rooted in love. How have you seen God's love provide a foundation for your life, helping you remain strong in the face of adversity? How does this love shape your relationships with others?
5. **Living Out God's Grace:** Ephesians 3:16 reminds us of God's abundant grace that strengthens believers. Reflect on a time when you experienced God's grace in a powerful way. How did

that experience inspire you to extend grace to others, and how has it influenced your relationship with God?

11

Philippians 3:16

Paul often uses running as a metaphor for the Christian life. In six different books, he compares the Christian journey to a footrace (Acts 20:24, 1 Cor 9:24, Gal 2:2, 2 Tim 4:7, Rom 9:16, Phil 3:14). However, when Paul reflects on all these "running" metaphors, he acknowledges that they pale in comparison to knowing Christ. In Philippians 3:8, Paul says that everything he once considered valuable is now "garbage" that he may gain Christ. He explains, in 3:7, that any gains he had in life are now considered a loss "because of the surpassing worth of knowing Christ Jesus, my Lord, for whose sake I have lost all things."

Imagine all your accomplishments—whether academic, athletic, or professional. Paul emphasizes that none of them compared to knowing Christ as Savior. Proverbs 4:18 reinforces this idea: "The path of the righteous is like the morning sun, shining ever brighter till the full light of day." The love of Christ is brighter than the morning sun, and no earthly achievement can surpass the light of His love.

Philippians 3:16 encourages perseverance and steadfastness in the Christian journey, stressing the importance of continual spiritual growth and transformation. Paul urges believers to "live up to what we have already attained." He carefully uses the word "we" to indicate that this spiritual journey is often taken in fellowship with other Christians. We do not walk alone but alongside our brothers and sisters in faith. Ecclesiastes 4:9-10 supports this concept, stating, "Two are better than one, because they have a good return for their labor: If either of them falls down, one can help the other up." Christian fellowship is just as important today as it was for the Philippians, as we encourage each other to stay on the right path and live out our faith together.

Every runner knows that in a race, they must focus their eyes ahead to avoid stumbling. An athlete must make a maximum effort to stay focused on the finish line. Similarly, Paul expresses his dissatisfaction with his spiritual progress, admitting that he had not yet achieved perfect focus. Despite being spiritually mature and growing in his faith in Jesus, Paul humbly acknowledges in Phil 3:12-13, "Not that I have already obtained all this... but I press on to take hold of that for which Christ Jesus took hold of me... I do not consider myself yet to have taken hold of it."

Paul's emphasis on his own imperfections serves to correct those in Philippi who believed they had already attained perfection, perhaps due to practices like circumcision, commandment-keeping, or ritual sacrifice. Paul wants the Christians in Philippi to understand that spiritual maturity is a marathon, not a sprint. Even the most devoted believers will still struggle with sin and fall at times.

The writer of Hebrews reinforces this idea of ongoing spiritual advancement, saying in 6:1 that spiritual growth is not stagnant but is always moving forward: "Therefore let us move beyond the elementary teachings about Christ and be taken forward to maturity." Spiritual maturity involves growing in wisdom, discernment, and the fruit of the Spirit from Galatians 5:22-23. As we grow spiritually, we increasingly reflect Christ in our thoughts, attitudes, and actions.

Paul also calls his brothers and sisters in Philippi to unite in the task of imitating him and encourages them to observe those who faithfully embody a Christ-shaped pattern of life. He knows that this attention to godly examples is crucial to the community's ability to live in a way that is worthy of the gospel, especially when surrounded by influences opposed to the self-giving love displayed on the cross.

Christian fellowship is a key opportunity for spiritual learning and growth as a community. Acts 2:42-47 describes how the early church lived in unity, sharing everything, and devoting themselves to the apostles' teachings. This community mindset is vital when a member of the body is struggling. Galatians 6:2 commands believers to "Carry each other's burdens, and in this way, you will fulfill the law of Christ." Just as early Christians supported one another, we too are called to help our fellow believers grow and persevere.

A biblical figure who exemplifies Philippians 3:16 is Ruth. Ruth's life is a powerful demonstration of perseverance, steadfast faith, and spiritual growth. She was a Moabite woman who, after the death of her husband, could have returned to her people and their gods. Yet, she displayed remarkable commitment by choosing to stay with her mother-in-law, Naomi, and follow the God of Israel. Ruth's declaration in Ruth 1:16 captures her determination: "Where you go, I will go, and where you stay, I will stay. Your people will be my people and your God my God." Ruth's decision to leave behind her old life and embrace Naomi's faith shows her steadfastness and desire for spiritual growth.

Ruth continued her new journey of faith by trusting God and obeying His guidance. She worked diligently in the fields of Boaz to provide for herself and Naomi. Her perseverance was rewarded by God, who blessed her in miraculous ways. Ruth 2:12 highlights this blessing: "May the Lord repay you for what you have done. May you be richly rewarded by the Lord, the God of Israel, under whose wings you have come to take refuge."

Ruth's life exemplifies Philippians 3:16—she lived up to what she had attained by pressing forward in faith and spiritual maturity. Her journey from a Moabite widow to the great-grandmother of King David, and part of Jesus' lineage, demonstrates how perseverance in faith can lead to profound spiritual growth and God's abundant blessings.

Applying Paul's letter and the example of Ruth, we are reminded to nurture and strengthen our relationship with Christ. We must adopt a growth-oriented mindset, recognizing that spiritual maturity is a lifelong journey. Like athletes in a race, we are called to run with humility and openness, allowing the Holy Spirit to continually work in us for the glory of Christ. Those who participate in Christ's life should align their minds and lives with His example, even as He endured the cross for the sake of others.

Journal Questions

1. **Perseverance in Faith:** Paul encourages believers to "live up to what we have already attained" and to keep pressing forward in their spiritual journey. Can you think of a time in your life when you felt challenged to persevere in your faith? How did you manage to stay focused on Christ despite difficulties?
2. **Community and Fellowship:** The narrative emphasizes the importance of Christian fellowship in our spiritual journey, as seen in both Paul's encouragement and the early church's example in Acts. How has fellowship with other believers helped you stay on track in your walk with Christ? How do you actively support others in their faith journey?
3. **Learning from Examples:** Paul calls believers to observe and imitate those who embody Christ-like lives, just as he encouraged the Philippians. Who in your life has served as a Christ-like example, and how has their life impacted your own spiritual growth and maturity?
4. **Endurance and Spiritual Growth:** Like Paul, Ruth persevered in her faith, even in challenging circumstances, and her story reflects growth and spiritual maturity. In what ways have your personal trials helped you grow spiritually? How has God rewarded your perseverance in faith?
5. **The Race of Faith:** The metaphor of running a race illustrates the Christian life as a continuous effort of growth and focus. What are some practical steps you take to keep your eyes focused on Christ, just as a runner focuses on the finish line? How

can you press forward in faith when faced with distractions or obstacles?

12

Colossians 3:16

Colossians 3:16 is found in a letter that Paul wrote while he was in prison, addressing a church that was struggling with confusion due to false teachings. These teachings blended Jewish legalism and pagan mysticism, pulling the believers away from the core truths of the gospel and undermining Christ's supremacy. This blending of ideologies led to significant doctrinal confusion and spiritual drift within the congregation.

In Chapter 3:1, Paul encourages the Colossians to "set your hearts on things above, where Christ is." He contrasts earthly and heavenly things, urging believers to "put off" their old selves, tied to worldly desires, and "put on" their new selves in Christ. This powerful imagery reflects the transformation that occurs when someone moves from darkness to light and from death to life in Jesus Christ, giving them a new identity.

Paul tells believers to "put to death" anything connected to their former sinful life. Since they are spiritually united with Christ, the power of sin over them is broken. This doesn't mean they won't be tempted, but through Christ, they now have the strength to resist it. Sin no longer holds dominion over them, and the earthly desires Paul lists—such as anger, malice, slander, and impurity—are like bait used by Satan to trap them in idolatry. Focusing on self-centered desires leads to putting oneself at the center instead of God.

Paul stresses that those who have died with Christ must also put to death all that separates them from Him. These earthly vices, once part of their former sinful lives, no longer define them. As believers, their new identity is shaped by Christ, who transforms their perceptions to focus on heavenly, not earthly, things.

Paul shifts his focus from behaviors to attitudes. He compares the sinful attitudes of anger, rage, malice, slander, and filthy language in Col 3:8 with the positive attitudes of compassion, kindness, humility, gentleness, and patience in Col 3:12. Paul uses the metaphor of "putting off" sinful attitudes like old clothes and "putting on" the virtues that reflect the image of God. By doing this, believers allow Christ's power and glory to shine through their lives.

Paul describes the new self as the person God intended them to be from the beginning. This renewal happens through Jesus, and as believers put off the old self, Col 3:10 tells believers they will begin to experience the renewal "in knowledge in the image of its Creator." This idea ties back to Genesis 1, where humankind was created in the image of God, but sin later marred that image. Paul's message is that through Christ, believers are being restored and made whole again.

Colossians 3:16 calls for the Word of Christ to dwell richly among believers. Paul emphasizes the transformative power of Scripture in both the hearts of individuals and the collective body of the church. This rich indwelling of the Word guides believers' thoughts and actions, renewing their minds, just as Romans 12:2 instructs believers to be transformed by the renewing of their minds. By letting the Word take root, believers are better equipped to live lives that honor God.

In addition to personal growth, Colossians 3:16 highlights the importance of mutual teaching, accountability, and encouragement within the Christian community. Proverbs 27:17 says, "As iron sharpens iron, so one person sharpens another." Paul envisions a community where believers teach and admonish one another in wisdom, singing psalms, hymns, and spiritual songs. Worship becomes an essential part of the communal life of faith, with gratitude overflowing in their hearts as they express their devotion to God.

The life of Ezra exemplifies the message of Colossians 3:16. Ezra was a priest and scribe who led the Jewish people in spiritual restoration after they returned from the Babylonian exile. In Nehemiah 8:1-3, Ezra stands before the assembly and reads from the Book of the Law from morning until midday. The people, who had been separated from their heritage for many years, listened intently to Ezra's teaching. Ezra wasn't just imparting knowledge—he was helping them let the Word of God dwell richly in their hearts, renewing their dedication to the Lord. When the people understood the Scriptures, they wept, realizing how far they had strayed from God. But Ezra encouraged them to rejoice, for rediscovering God's Word was a moment of renewal and restoration. This mirrors the spirit of Colossians 3:16, where worship and gratitude flow naturally from a deep understanding of God's Word.

Ezra's dedication to teaching God's Word brought transformation to the community, just as Paul urges in Colossians. As believers, we are called to let God's Word dwell richly within us so that it shapes our lives and brings renewal. Joshua 1:8 reminds us to meditate on the Word of God day and night, allowing it to influence our thoughts, decisions, and behavior. Engaging with Scripture both individually and corporately creates an atmosphere of spiritual growth, love, and accountability within the church. Finally, Colossians 3:16 encourages believers to actively participate in corporate worship. Through psalms, hymns, and spiritual songs, we express our gratitude, praise, and devotion to God. This collective worship fosters unity in the body of Christ and strengthens our faith, reminding us of God's faithfulness. Worship, teaching, and Scripture all work together to renew and transform us, building up the church as we grow in faith and maturity.

Journal Questions

1. **Renewal Through Scripture:** Paul urges believers to let the Word of Christ dwell richly among them. How has regular en-

gagement with Scripture transformed your life, guiding your thoughts and actions? Can you think of a specific time when the Word of God brought renewal to a difficult situation in your life?

2. **Putting Off the Old Self:** Paul talks about putting off sinful behaviors and attitudes to embrace the new self in Christ. What are some "old self" attitudes or behaviors you've needed to let go of, and how has embracing Christ's character helped you grow spiritually?

3. **The Power of Worship:** Colossians 3:16 emphasizes worship through psalms, hymns, and spiritual songs. How has participating in corporate worship helped strengthen your faith and bring a deeper sense of gratitude and joy in your walk with God?

4. **Mutual Edification and Accountability:** Paul stresses the importance of teaching and admonishing one another within the church community. How has being part of a church or small group provided you with encouragement and accountability? How do you contribute to the spiritual growth of others in your community?

5. **Ezra's Example of Leadership:** Ezra helped restore the Jewish community by reading and teaching the Word of God, leading to renewal. In what ways can you or have you helped others grow in their faith by sharing God's Word? How can you apply Ezra's dedication to teaching and encouraging others within your own community?

13

1 Thessalonians

Paul's letter to the Thessalonians doesn't include a 3:16 verse, but it centers around an important message to a young church he had previously established during one of his missionary journeys. The inspiration for this letter came from a report Paul received at a challenging time in his ministry. He had faced serious opposition in Philippi, Thessalonica, and Berea, and experienced limited success in Athens, which must have been discouraging.

However, when Timothy returned from Thessalonica with news about the church's perseverance and faith, it was a turning point for Paul. Even though Paul had to leave Thessalonica sooner than planned, Timothy's report showed Paul how God's blessing had been present in his work there. Paul's joy and thanksgiving for the Thessalonians' faithfulness can be felt throughout his letter.

Paul acknowledges the difficulties and rejection the new believers are experiencing, reminding them of Jesus' words from John 16:33: "In this world you will have trouble. But take heart! I have overcome the world." Paul had personally faced similar opposition, with Jews and Gentiles in the region strongly opposing his message. The persecution was so severe that after Paul left Thessalonica, his opponents followed him to Berea to continue stirring up opposition.

Despite these challenges, Paul spends much of the letter expressing his gratitude for the Thessalonians' perseverance and providing further guidance on how to live faithfully in a hostile environment. He emphasizes holy living and readiness for Christ's return, something the Thessalonians eagerly awaited.

Paul's message to the Thessalonians extends to all believers today. He teaches that the Christian life involves faith, love, and hope, always in light of the past and looking toward the future. He reflects on his time with the Thessalonians, caring for them like "a nursing mother cares for her children," and reminds them of their early faith in the gospel. Even in the face of trials, the Thessalonians have grown in faith, which brings Paul immense joy.

Paul encourages them to continue living in holiness, keeping Christ's return in view. He reassures them of the certainty of this return, urging them to live with purpose and purity. 1 Thessalonians 4:16-17 teaches that "the Lord himself will come down from heaven" and believers should live in readiness for that day. This future hope motivates believers to live with constant awareness of eternity.

For believers today, Paul's letter offers valuable lessons about enduring faith and steadfast hope in anticipation of Christ's return. His message encourages us to trust God through trials, knowing He is faithful. The reminder of Christ's return is not just to inform us about the future, but to transform how we live now.

Paul also emphasizes the importance of Christian fellowship and mutual support, reminding us that community is essential for spiritual growth. As Hebrews 10:24-25 urges, "spur one another on toward love and good deeds, not giving up meeting together." Christian accountability strengthens us, especially during challenging times.

Hannah, from the Old Testament, exemplifies the message of 1 Thessalonians about living with faith, prayer, and gratitude. In 1 Samuel 1-2, despite her deep sorrow over being childless, Hannah continued to seek God, praying with great faith. Her persistent prayer mirrors Paul's call in 1 Thessalonians 5:16-18 to "rejoice always, pray continually, give thanks in all circumstances." When God answered her prayers, Hannah responded with a heart full of worship, as seen in her prayer of thanksgiving in 1 Samuel 2:1-10.

Hannah's life shows us that prayer, faith, and gratitude can sustain us during tough times. She is a powerful example of how to trust in God's plan, even when circumstances seem difficult. Like the Thessalonians, we are called to hold on to hope, faith, and love, always trusting in Christ's promises.

In conclusion, 1 Thessalonians highlights the enduring power of faith, hope, and love. Paul encourages believers to stay steadfast in faith, eagerly await Christ's return, and show love to others. Romans 8:18 offers hope: "I consider that our present sufferings are not worth comparing with the glory that will be revealed in us." By embracing this message, believers can confidently face life's challenges, knowing that present struggles are temporary, and their ultimate victory is secure in Christ.

Journal Questions

1. **Persevering Through Trials:** Like the Thessalonians, Paul faced severe opposition and discouragement. Reflect on a time when you experienced difficulty or rejection of your beliefs or values. How did your faith help you persevere through those challenges, and how did God's faithfulness sustain you?
2. **Living in Anticipation of Christ's Return:** Paul emphasized that Christ's return is certain and encourages us to live in readiness and holiness. How does the hope of Christ's second coming impact the way you live your daily life? In what areas do you feel called to live with more intentionality and purpose?
3. **Faith, Love, and Hope in Your Journey:** Paul commends the Thessalonians for their faith, love, and hope in Christ, even in the face of adversity. Reflect on how these three virtues are present in your own life. How do you maintain a balance between faith, love, and hope, especially during difficult times?
4. **The Importance of Christian Fellowship:** Paul stresses the value of community and mutual support in the Christian life. How has fellowship with other believers encouraged or

strengthened you during difficult seasons? What steps can you take to better support and encourage others in your faith community?

5. **Learning from Hannah's Example:** Like Hannah, who prayed persistently and gave thanks even in sorrow, 1 Thessalonians 5:16-18 calls us to "rejoice always, pray continually, give thanks in all circumstances." How do you practice prayer, joy, and gratitude during times of hardship? In what ways can you cultivate a deeper attitude of thanksgiving, even when facing challenges?

14

2 Thessalonians 3:16

After receiving joyful news from Timothy about the steadfastness of the church in Thessalonica, Paul sent them a letter of encouragement to help them through the suffering they were enduring from those who opposed them. He also provided guidance on living a holy life and instructed them to live in anticipation of Christ's return. It's believed that Timothy shared these concerns with Paul, and because Paul's presence would have been too disruptive for their young church, he chose to offer his support in writing.

Not long after Paul sent the positive and uplifting letter of 1 Thessalonians, new issues arose. While the Thessalonians continued to grow in faith and remain loyal to Christ, some confusion had entered the church. False teachings about the "day of the Lord" were circulating, leading some believers to stop working, possibly thinking Christ's return was imminent.

Paul quickly addressed this concern in 2 Thessalonians 2:2 where he warns against the false claim that "the day of the Lord had already come." He explains that before Christ's return, there would be a "man of lawlessness," or Satan's agent, who would cause destruction and deceive many with false signs and wonders. Paul urges the Thessalonians to avoid becoming passive or fanatical about Christ's return and to stay grounded in their faith.

Paul encourages the Thessalonians to stand firm in their faith as the "first fruits" of the Holy Spirit's work, reminding them to hold on to the Gospel and its promises of hope and peace. He asks for prayer for continued growth of the Church, urging the believers to follow his example by staying faithful and doing what is right.

As Paul begins to close his second letter, 2 Thessalonians 3:16 contains his blessing of peace: "Now may the Lord of peace himself give you peace at all times and in every way." This peace is a gift from God that remains constant, no matter what trials or hardships believers face. Unlike peace that humans try to create, God's peace is unshakable and enduring.

One of the reasons for the anxiety in Thessalonica was the division caused by false teachings. These teachings led some believers to become idle, while others were anxious and confused. Paul's call for peace in this letter was not just for individuals but for the entire church, urging them to come together in unity and harmony.

The idea of peace in this context reflects the biblical concept of shalom, a Hebrew word that encompasses wholeness, completeness, and well-being. Hezekiah, the king of Judah, exemplifies the message of 2 Thessalonians 3:16, "Now may the Lord of peace himself give you peace at all times and in every way. The Lord be with all of you." Hezekiah's life, particularly during the Assyrian invasion, displays how God's peace can guard a leader's heart even when surrounded by fear and overwhelming threats.

During Hezekiah's reign, the Assyrian king Sennacherib laid siege to Jerusalem. Sennacherib sent messengers to taunt Hezekiah and the people, mocking their trust in God and threatening to destroy them, just as the Assyrians had destroyed other nations explained in 2 Kings 18:17-35. Despite the immense pressure and fear that this brought to the city, Hezekiah responded by seeking peace in God's presence rather than reacting in panic.

Hezekiah went to the temple, spread Sennacherib's threatening letter before the Lord, and prayed for deliverance. In 2 Kings 19:15-19, Hezekiah acknowledges God's sovereignty over all the earth and asks Him to deliver Judah so that all nations would know that the Lord alone is God. This act of faith in God's power brought peace amidst the siege.

God answered Hezekiah's prayer through the prophet Isaiah, who assured him that God would defend the city. That night, the angel of the Lord struck down 185,000 Assyrian soldiers, and Sennacherib withdrew (2 Kings 19:35-36). Hezekiah experienced God's peace, much like the promise in Isaiah 26:3, "You will keep in perfect peace those whose minds are steadfast, because they trust in you."

Hezekiah's story reflects 2 Thessalonians 3:16 by showing that God's peace, which surpasses all understanding, can protect and sustain His people even in the face of the greatest challenges.

Paul closes the letter by echoing his opening words, referencing the grace of the Lord Jesus Christ. 2 Thessalonians 3:16 serves as a powerful reminder that God desires His people to experience peace in all circumstances. It offers comfort and assurance during uncertain times, highlighting the lasting presence of God's peace. Peace be with you, the reader.

Journal Questions

1. **Experiencing God's Peace:** Reflect on a time in your life when you felt overwhelmed by challenges or uncertainty. How did you experience God's peace, like Hezekiah did when facing the Assyrian invasion? What steps did you take to find peace in God's presence, and how did this strengthen your faith?
2. **Dealing with False Teachings:** Paul addressed the confusion caused by false teachings in the Thessalonian church. Have you ever faced a situation where misinformation or doubt caused confusion in your faith? How did you overcome it, and how can grounding yourself in Scripture help you remain firm in your beliefs?
3. **Standing Firm in Faith:** Paul encouraged the Thessalonians to stand firm in their faith amidst challenges. What areas of your life challenge your faith today, and how can you continue

to persevere and stand firm, knowing that God offers you His peace and strength?

4. **Unity in the Church:** Paul's call for peace was not only for individuals but for the whole church community. How can you contribute to promoting peace and unity within your church or community when conflicts or misunderstandings arise?

5. **Living in Anticipation of Christ's Return:** The Thessalonians were eager but sometimes confused about the return of Christ. How can the promise of Christ's return motivate you to live with purpose, holiness, and hope today? How does this anticipation shape your daily life and decisions?

15

1 Timothy 3:16

1 Timothy, together with 2 Timothy and Titus, is part of what is known as the Pastoral Epistles. These letters focus on providing guidance for Christian leadership. This letter in particular was written to support Timothy in his role as a leader, instructing him to teach sound doctrine, show love, and emphasize God's role as Savior.

When Paul arrived in Lystra, he heard about a young man named Timothy, who had been taught the Scriptures by his mother, Eunice, and grandmother, Lois. Paul and Timothy quickly formed a strong bond, and Paul referred to him as "my true son in the faith" in 1 Timothy 1:2. They traveled and ministered together across various regions, and when Paul left Timothy in Ephesus to continue working with the church there, this letter was written to provide further guidance and encouragement to Timothy in his role as a Christian leader. Timothy's example as a church leader is also a model for Christian leaders today.

Within this letter, we find 1 Timothy 3:16, a powerful statement summarizing the mystery of godliness revealed through Jesus Christ. This verse, composed in six lines, explains a core belief of the Christian faith. The term "mystery" refers to something once hidden but now revealed, which in this case is the gospel message of Jesus Christ. The verse begins with, "He appeared in the flesh," affirming that Jesus, the eternal Son of God, became fully human. The incarnation of Jesus is central to Christian belief, demonstrating God's deep love and grace by identifying fully with humanity. Jesus, who performed miracles, taught with authority, and experienced hunger, fatigue, and sorrow without sin.

Scriptures such as Isaiah 7:14 prophesied, "The virgin will conceive and give birth to a son." While John 1:14 says, "The Word became flesh and made his dwelling among us." These verses, from Old Testament prophecy to New Testament fulfillment, reinforce that Jesus was both fully human and fully divine. This foundational belief affirms that Jesus is the mediator between God and humanity, perfectly bridging the gap caused by sin.

The phrase "vindicated by the Spirit" refers to how the Holy Spirit affirmed Jesus' ministry. At His baptism, the Spirit descended on Him like a dove (Matt 3:16). Jesus' sinlessness and the miracles He performed, empowered by the Spirit, are further evidence of this divine confirmation. As Jesus drove out demons, it is recorded that He said, "But if it is by the Spirit of God that I drive out demons, then the kingdom of God has come upon you."

The line "was seen by angels" recalls the many times angels were present in Jesus' life. Angels announced His birth to Mary and Joseph, sang at His birth, ministered to Him after His temptation in the wilderness, and were present at His resurrection to proclaim that He had risen. Finally, at Jesus' ascension, Luke says in Acts 1:11, angels appeared again, assuring His disciples that He would return in the same way He was taken up.

The phrase "was taken up in glory" refers to Jesus' ascension to heaven. This moment marked His return to His heavenly throne, where He reigns with all authority. Hebrews 7:25 emphasizes that Jesus now intercedes for us, seated at the right hand of God. The ascension is not only a sign of His divine authority but also a promise that He will return. For believers, it brings assurance that Jesus reigns and will return in glory to make all things new.

Samuel exemplifies the message of 1 Timothy 3:16. Samuel, born as an answer to his mother Hannah's fervent prayers, was dedicated to God from birth and grew up serving in the temple under Eli. His life was marked by deep faith, godliness, and obedience to God's calling. In 1 Samuel 3:19, we read, "The Lord was with Samuel as he grew up, and he let none of Samuel's words fall to the ground." This closeness to God and his role as a prophet reflect Samuel's embodiment of godliness, as described in 1 Timothy 3:16.

Samuel played a pivotal role in anointing Israel's first kings, Saul and David, pointing toward God's plan of redemption. His prophetic ministry foreshadowed the coming of Jesus, the true King, who "appeared in the flesh." Samuel's dedication to God's plan reflects the values of Micah 6:8, "To act justly and to love mercy and to walk humbly with your God." His life mirrors the godliness and devotion to God's purposes that is stated in 1 Timothy 3:16.

1 Timothy 3:16 calls believers to live in a way that reflects the truth of Christ's incarnation and exaltation. It encourages us to imitate Christ's humility, showing sacrificial love, and extending grace to others. It also urges believers to share the gospel message, proclaiming Christ's life, death, resurrection, and ascension to those around them. As we live in anticipation of Christ's return, this verse reminds us to shape our lives and priorities around the hope of His coming, inviting others to experience God's love and mercy through Jesus Christ.

Journal Questions

1. **Reflecting on the Incarnation:** 1 Timothy 3:16 speaks of Christ "appearing in the flesh." What does Jesus' willingness to take on human form mean to you personally? How does His identification with humanity impact the way you understand God's love and grace?
2. **Experiencing God's Vindication:** The phrase "vindicated by the Spirit" refers to how the Holy Spirit affirmed Jesus' ministry. Reflect on a time in your life when you felt the Holy Spirit's guidance or confirmation. How did that experience strengthen your faith or lead you closer to God?

3. **Living with Anticipation:** Jesus was "taken up in glory" and now reigns with all authority. How does the knowledge of Jesus' current reign and His eventual return influence the way you live your daily life? What steps can you take to live with more intentional anticipation of Christ's return?
4. **Responding to God's Revelation:** 1 Timothy 3:16 reveals the mystery of godliness that was once hidden but is now made known through Christ. How does this unfolding of God's plan, from prophecy to fulfillment, inspire your faith? In what ways can you deepen your understanding of God's Word to grow in your knowledge of Him?
5. **Emulating Godliness:** Samuel is an example of godliness and devotion to God's plan, as reflected in 1 Timothy 3:16. Think about a time when you had to follow God's plan, even if it was difficult. How did your obedience and faithfulness in that situation reflect Samuel's example, and what did you learn about godly living through it?

16

2 Timothy 3:16

2 Timothy, likely the final letter written by the Apostle Paul, was written during his imprisonment in Rome, shortly before his martyrdom. Along with 1 Timothy and Titus, this letter is part of what is known as the Pastoral Epistles. These letters focus on providing guidance for church leadership, sound teaching, and good works. However, 2 Timothy is less focused on church structure and more centered on Paul's personal example of faithfulness, perseverance, and devotion to the gospel. Paul wrote this letter to encourage his young disciple, Timothy, to remain strong and steadfast in the face of challenges.

Timothy was facing difficulties as a church leader; especially as false teachings were spreading within the Christian community. Paul knew that Timothy needed support and encouragement, so he reminded him of the foundational truth of Scripture in 2 Timothy 3:16. This verse reassures Timothy and all believers today that the Bible is the ultimate source of wisdom, correction, and righteousness. It affirms that Scripture is not only a source of knowledge but also the foundation of transformation for all who follow Christ.

2 Timothy 3:16 is one of the most important verses in the New Testament regarding the nature of Scripture. It touches on what faith means for believers today. Every word in the Bible affects how Christians live out their faith and make decisions. In this long, typical Pauline sentence, Paul communicates two vital truths about Scripture.

First, he declares that all Scripture is "God-breathed," confirming its divine origin. Second, he outlines its purpose: to teach, rebuke, correct, and train in righteousness.

The phrase "God-breathed" highlights the divine source of Scripture, meaning that it comes directly from God, though it was written by human hands. This stresses that while humans wrote the words, the Holy Spirit guided them. By stating that all Scripture is "God-breathed," Paul assures believers that the Bible is trustworthy, accurate, and without error in its teaching. Because God inspired it, the Bible is not just an ancient book—it is God's personal communication to humanity. Just as God breathed life into Adam in Genesis 2:7, He breathes life into us through His Word. In Job 33:4, it says, "The Spirit of God has made me; the breath of the Almighty gives me life."

Peter supports this in 2 Peter 1:21, where he writes, "For prophecy never had its origin in the human will, but prophets, though human, spoke from God as they were carried along by the Holy Spirit." This confirms that God used human authors to reveal His truth while ensuring its accuracy. Even Jesus acknowledged the authority of Scripture when He responded to Satan's temptation in Matthew 4:4 by saying, "Man shall not live on bread alone, but on every word that comes from the mouth of God."

Through Scripture, God reveals His character, His will, and His plan for salvation. As believers study Scripture, they enter into communion with God, allowing His Word to shape their thoughts, decisions, and actions. The Bible equips believers for every good work, 2 Timothy 3:17, guiding them not only in understanding God's will but in living it out.

From Genesis to Revelation, the Bible reveals who God is and how He interacts with His creation. In the Old Testament, God establishes His covenant with Israel and gives instructions for holy living. In the New Testament, God reveals Himself most fully in Jesus Christ, who embodies God's redemptive plan for humanity. Jesus shows that salvation can only come through Him, as Scripture reminds us in Proverbs 3:5-6: "Trust in the Lord with all your heart and lean not on your own understanding; in all your ways submit to him, and he will make your paths straight."

Apollos exemplifies the message of 2 Timothy 3:16, which teaches that all Scripture is God-breathed and useful for teaching, rebuking, correcting, and training in righteousness. Apollos, an early church teacher, used Scripture to teach others about Jesus and to correct misunderstandings.

Acts 18:24-28 introduces Apollos as a learned person with a deep knowledge of the Scriptures. He accurately taught about Jesus, even though he only knew about John's baptism. Apollos taught boldly, using the Old Testament to prove that Jesus was the Messiah. His teaching aligned with 2 Timothy 3:16, as he used Scripture to instruct others in truth.

Yet, Apollos still needed correction. When Priscilla and Aquila heard him, they explained the way of God more fully to him (Acts 18:26). Apollos' willingness to accept correction demonstrates the importance of humility, which is part of the rebuke and correction mentioned in 2 Timothy 3:16. After receiving further instruction, Apollos became an even more effective preacher of the gospel, continuing to use Scripture to show that Jesus was the Messiah (Acts 18:28).

We are called to submit to God's Word, allowing it to teach, correct, and transform us. By studying Scripture, meditating on its truths, and applying its principles, we grow in faith and wisdom. Joshua 1:8 encourages us to meditate on God's Word day and night, ensuring that it remains central in our lives. By consistently engaging with Scripture, we are better equipped to face life's challenges and live according to God's will.

Journal Questions

1. **Understanding the Divine Inspiration of Scripture:** Reflect on the concept of Scripture being "God-breathed" as described in 2 Timothy 3:16. How does knowing that the Bible is divinely inspired change the way you approach reading and

studying it in your daily life? What steps can you take to engage more deeply with God's Word?

2. **Applying Scripture to Life:** 2 Timothy 3:16 highlights the Bible's purpose for teaching, rebuking, correcting, and training in righteousness. Can you think of a time when reading Scripture challenged your thinking or corrected a behavior? How did applying God's Word lead to growth or transformation in that situation?

3. **Humility in Correction:** Apollos, a gifted teacher, accepted corrections from Priscilla and Aquila in Acts 18:26. How do you respond to correction, whether it comes from Scripture or through others? What can you learn from Apollos's humility in receiving guidance, and how can this attitude help you grow spiritually?

4. **Engaging with God's Word for Spiritual Growth:** Joshua 1:8 encourages believers to meditate on Scripture day and night. What practices do you have in place to consistently engage with God's Word? How can you make Scripture a more central part of your daily routine to grow in wisdom, faith, and righteousness?

5. **The Transformative Power of Scripture:** 2 Timothy 3:16 reminds us that Scripture equips believers for every good work. In what areas of your life do you need God's guidance or correction right now? How can you allow the transformative power of Scripture to help you navigate these areas with wisdom and faith?

17

Titus

The letter to Titus, one of the three Pastoral Epistles, is brief but rich in its teachings about leadership, sound doctrine, and godly living. Titus, a trusted companion of Paul, was sent to Crete to establish and organize church leadership there. Paul wanted to ensure that these churches were built on a strong foundation of truth and effective leadership. Right from the start of the letter, Paul sets the tone by focusing on authority, grace, sound teaching, and preaching—qualities essential for Christian leaders, both then and now.

Paul's first task for Titus was to appoint elders in every town. He knew that having strong, trustworthy leaders was essential for building and maintaining a healthy church. Paul gave clear instructions on what kind of person an elder should be, stating in Titus 1:6, that an elder must be "blameless, faithful to his wife, and have children who are believers and not open to the charge of being wild and disobedient". He then goes into detail about what being blameless means and adds that elders must hold firmly to sound doctrine. Elders are expected not only to encourage others in their faith but also to confront false teachings and correct those who are going astray.

Like in his letters to Timothy, Paul urged Titus to rebuke false teachers who were causing problems within the church. Sound doctrine is the bedrock of the Christian faith, and Paul wanted to make sure that the truth of the gospel was taught clearly and with conviction. In the same way, churches today need to be rooted in the Word of God, both to defend against false teachings and to equip believers to understand God's will and live by it.

Sound doctrine, however, is not just about what we believe; it must also shape how we live. Paul emphasized that true faith leads to a transformed life, where actions match beliefs. Jesus himself taught this principle in Matthew 7:24-27, where he compares those who listen to his words and put them into practice to a wise man who builds his house on the rock. Those who ignore his teachings are like a foolish man who builds on sand, with disastrous results. A life built on the solid foundation of Christ and his teachings will stand firm, even in difficult times.

Paul also reminds Titus that living a godly life is only possible through the grace of God. In Titus 2:14, he writes that Jesus "gave himself for us to redeem us from all wickedness and to purify for himself a people that are his very own, eager to do what is good." As believers, we are redeemed to live in a way that reflects righteousness, justice, and love for others. The good works we do are not just outward actions but are evidence of the inward transformation that has taken place because of God's grace. As James 2:26 says, "Faith without works is dead." This aligns with Paul's message that we should pursue good works as a demonstration of our faith and as a witness to the world.

A biblical figure who exemplifies the message of Titus is Barnabas. Known as the "Son of Encouragement" from Acts 4:36, Barnabas was a key leader in the early church. Like Titus, he was responsible for strengthening and encouraging new believers, establishing strong church leadership, and teaching sound doctrine. Acts 11:22-24 tells us when the apostles heard of Gentiles coming to faith in Antioch, they sent Barnabas to ensure the community was grounded in truth and good works, much like Titus was tasked with in Crete.

Barnabas also mentored Paul, guiding him early in his ministry and helping to strengthen the church in Antioch, just as Proverbs 27:17 says, "As iron sharpens iron, so one person sharpens another." His role in the early church aligns with Paul's instructions to Titus, as

Barnabas encouraged believers to remain true to their faith and live lives of integrity and good deeds.

Additionally, Barnabas took John Mark under his wing, even after Mark had previously deserted Paul and Barnabas on a missionary journey. Despite Paul's reluctance to take Mark on further trips, Barnabas saw potential in Mark and worked to restore him, showing how Barnabas lived out the call to encourage and mentor others, just as Titus was called to do in Crete. Barnabas's willingness to restore Mark reflects the heart of Paul's message in Titus about the importance of second chances, mercy, and maintaining unity within the church.

Paul's letter to Titus continues to offer timeless guidance on leadership, doctrine, and living out one's faith. Paul's instructions to establish strong, biblically sound leadership in the churches of Crete are just as relevant today. It challenges us to reflect on our own leadership qualities—are we leading with integrity, wisdom, and humility? Moreover, it serves as a call to embody Christ-like leadership, ensuring that our actions reflect God's character.

In Paul's final instructions from Titus 3:14, he emphasizes that good works should be the natural outflow of our faith, not a means of salvation but as the fruit of a transformed life. Christians should be actively involved in serving others, showing kindness, and working for justice, demonstrating Christ's love to those around us. As 2 Corinthians 5:17 reminds us, "If anyone is in Christ, the new creation has come: The old has gone, the new is here!" Our good works are a reflection of the new life we have in Christ.

Journal Questions

1. **Leadership in the Church:** Reflect on Paul's instructions to Titus about appointing elders with strong moral character and sound doctrine (Titus 1:5-9). What qualities do you think are essential in church leadership today, and how can you cultivate these traits in your own life or community?

2. **Living Out Sound Doctrine:** Titus 2:14 reminds us that Christ redeemed us so we can be "eager to do what is good." How does your faith impact your daily actions and decisions? What practical steps can you take to ensure that your conduct aligns with the teachings of the gospel?
3. **Facing False Teachings:** Paul tasked Titus with addressing false teachings in the church (Titus 1:10-16). How can you discern truth from falsehood in your own faith journey? What role does sound doctrine play in helping you navigate conflicting messages in today's world?
4. **Encouraging Others:** Barnabas is known as the "Son of Encouragement" and mentored key figures like Paul and John Mark. Reflect on the time when you received encouragement from someone. How did it impact your faith, and how can you become a source of encouragement to others in your community?
5. **The Role of Good Works:** Paul emphasizes the importance of good works as a natural outflow of faith (Titus 3:14). How do your actions reflect your relationship with God? What opportunities do you have in your daily life to serve others and demonstrate Christ's love?

18

Philemon

It's amazing how much can be said in just 25 verses and 335 words. This is Paul's letter to his friend Philemon. While there are different theories about the exact background of this letter, one thing is certain: Paul, who is usually very detailed in his letters, leaves out many specifics in this one. What we do know is that Paul is in prison, Onesimus is with him, and Paul is asking Philemon to welcome Onesimus back not as a slave, but as a brother in Christ.

One possible explanation for this situation is that in Roman times, if a slave got into trouble with their master, they could seek help from a trusted friend of the master. In this case, Onesimus may have gone to Paul for help and, during that time, became a Christian. For Paul, this changed the relationship between Onesimus and Philemon. Instead of being master and slave, Paul now sees them as brothers in Christ, and he asks Philemon to see it that way, too.

Looking deeper into this brief letter, we find foundational Christian beliefs. One of the main themes is love and grace. After Paul's typical greeting, verse 5 says he thanks Philemon for his "love for all his holy people and your faith in the Lord Jesus." Paul's letter shows how love and grace can transform lives. Paul, even while in prison, reaches out in love to help his brother Onesimus, showing that grace knows no boundaries.

Instead of commanding Philemon, Paul appeals to him in love, asking him to treat Onesimus as a brother. Paul also expresses his gratitude for Philemon's faith, saying it has encouraged him and brought him joy. This sets the tone for Paul's request: that Philemon's love for his fellow believers should extend to Onesimus.

This message of love and grace is found throughout Scripture. In Ephesians 4:32, Paul says, "Be kind and compassionate to one another, forgiving each other, just as in Christ God forgave you." Paul's request to Philemon highlights the radical nature of Christian love, which goes beyond holding grudges and instead mirrors God's boundless grace.

Paul's letter also focuses on forgiveness and reconciliation, two key aspects of Christian faith. He urges Philemon to forgive Onesimus and welcome him back not as a slave but as a beloved brother in Christ. Even though Paul could use his authority as an apostle to command Philemon, he chooses to appeal in love, showing how the gospel breaks down barriers like status and power. Paul hopes Philemon will see Onesimus as an equal, a reflection of how Christ reconciles us to God.

Forgiveness is a major theme throughout Jesus' teachings. In Matthew 6:12-14, Jesus emphasizes the importance of forgiving others as we have been forgiven. Paul's appeal for reconciliation reflects this priority, reminding us of how Christ's forgiveness transforms relationships.

Jonathan, the son of King Saul, exemplifies the spirit of Philemon through his loyalty, willingness to reconcile, and selfless love. Jonathan's friendship with David is a powerful example of sacrificial love and peacemaking, much like Paul's appeal for Philemon to forgive Onesimus. In 1 Samuel 18:3-4, Jonathan made a covenant with David, even though he was the rightful heir to Saul's throne. He supported David, just as Paul urged Philemon to support Onesimus, choosing love over status or power.

In 1 Samuel 19:4-6, Jonathan also worked as a peacemaker between David and Saul, just as Paul seeks to bring Philemon and Onesimus together. Jonathan's loyalty and commitment to reconciliation reflect the same values that Paul encourages in his letter to Philemon, emphasizing the importance of brotherhood and peace.

In Proverbs 17:17, we are reminded that "A friend loves at all times, and a brother is born for a time of adversity." Jonathan lived this out by standing with David through difficult times, and Philemon is challenged to do the same for Onesimus.

Paul's letter to Philemon provides a powerful lesson for us today. It encourages us to think about how we extend grace and forgiveness in our own relationships. Just as Paul urged Philemon to welcome Onesimus as a brother, we are called to forgive and seek reconciliation with those who have wronged us. As we follow these principles, we grow spiritually and show the world the true nature of God's love and grace.

Journal Questions

1. **Understanding Christian Love and Grace:** In Paul's letter, he asks Philemon to show love and grace to Onesimus. Reflect on the time when you had to extend grace to someone who wronged you. How did your faith influence your response, and what impact did it have on your relationship?
2. **Embodying Forgiveness and Reconciliation:** Paul advocates for forgiveness and reconciliation between Philemon and Onesimus. Are there relationships in your life where forgiveness is needed? How might practicing reconciliation, as Paul encouraged, transform that relationship?
3. **The Gospel's Impact on Relationships:** Paul urges Philemon to see Onesimus not as a slave, but as a brother in Christ. How does the gospel challenge us to view and treat others, especially those who may hold a different social status or background than us?
4. **Sacrificial Love and Peacemaking:** Jonathan's loyalty to David, even when it was risky, reflects the kind of sacrificial love that Paul appeals for. When have you had to stand by

someone during a difficult time, like Jonathan did for David? How did it reflect your commitment to Christ-like love?
5. **The Role of Christian Fellowship:** Paul emphasizes the unity shared among believers, regardless of past wrongs or social divisions. How can you foster stronger bonds of fellowship within your church or community, ensuring that grace, love, and forgiveness are central to your relationships?

19

Hebrews 3:16

Although we don't know who wrote Hebrews, it's clear the letter was meant for Jewish Christians. The writer seems very familiar with the Old Testament and knows how to present strong arguments, much like the ancient Greeks. While we don't know the author or the exact time it was written, this doesn't affect the message of the letter. The main theme of Hebrews is the saving power of Jesus' death and resurrection.

In Hebrews Chapter 3, the author uses an example that all Jews and Jewish Christians knew well: the Exodus. This example shows that Jesus is greater than Moses, a deeply respected figure in Jewish faith. The author explains how the Israelites' unbelief during the Exodus kept them from entering the Promised Land, using this as a lesson for Christians to stay faithful. The writer encourages believers to hold onto their faith, even when life gets tough, and not make the same mistakes the Israelites did.

If we look deeper into the story of the Exodus, we can see that the temptations the Israelites faced are similar to those Jesus faced in the wilderness. After Jesus was baptized and the Holy Spirit came upon Him, He was led into the wilderness for 40 days, where Satan tempted Him. Satan waited until Jesus was weak from hunger and exhaustion before trying to lead Him astray.

Satan tempted Jesus in three main ways: by asking Him to turn stones into bread, by challenging Him to test God's protection by jumping off the Temple, and by offering Jesus all the kingdoms of the world if He would worship Satan. In each temptation, Jesus resisted by quoting Scripture from the book of Deuteronomy (Deut. 8:3, 6:16, 6:13), showing His trust in God.

Similarly, in the Exodus story, the Israelites faced these types of temptations. When they were hungry in the desert, they grumbled against God, but He provided manna and quail (Exodus 16). When they were thirsty, they tested God at Meribah (Exodus 17), much like Satan tried to get Jesus to test God's protection. Later, when Moses was gone for a long time on Mount Sinai, the Israelites asked Aaron to make a golden calf for them to worship (Exodus 32). This mirrors the third temptation, where Satan offered Jesus worldly power in exchange for worship.

Hebrews 3:16 is a rhetorical question that reminds the readers that, just like their ancestors, they have heard God's Word, yet they are still at risk of rebelling. The verse serves as a warning about the serious consequences of unbelief. Even though the Israelites saw God's miracles, they rebelled during their journey. Jesus, who is greater than Moses, did not fall into these temptations, but the Israelites did.

The author of Hebrews knew that the Jewish Christians were facing persecution and were tempted to abandon their faith in Christ. By pointing to the Exodus story, the author encourages these believers to keep trusting Jesus. Turning away from Christ would be as disastrous as the Israelites turning away from God. Their lack of faith led to their punishment, causing them to wander in the desert for 40 years.

This verse emphasizes that the Israelites missed out on entering God's rest because of their unbelief. For Christians, this serves as a reminder that faith is more than a one-time statement; it's a lifelong commitment to trust God through every challenge. Hebrews 12:1-2 urges us to "run with perseverance the race marked out for us, fixing our eyes on Jesus, the pioneer and perfecter of faith." Perseverance helps believers grow spiritually and rely more deeply on God's grace.

Caleb, a figure from the Old Testament, represents the message of Hebrews 3:16. He showed unwavering faith in God's promises, unlike the rest of his generation, who rebelled against God. In Numbers 13, Caleb was one of the spies sent to explore the Promised Land, and while most of the spies gave a fearful report, Caleb trusted God's power and urged the people to go and take the land. Because of Caleb's faithfulness, Numbers 14:24, says God promised that he, unlike the others, would enter the Promised Land.

Caleb's example stands in contrast to the Israelites' disobedience, much like the warning in Hebrews 3:16. He remained faithful, obedient, and full of trust in God's promises, setting an example for us today.

Hebrews 3:16 offers us a challenge: to regularly check our own hearts and our trust in God's Word. Just as the Israelites and Jesus faced temptations, we too will face challenges in our faith. But like Jesus, we are called to persevere and trust in God's Word. Even though humanity's struggle with temptation started all the way back with Adam and Eve, we are reminded through Scripture to resist and trust in God.

Adam and Eve, in Genesis Chapter Three, faced three similar temptations as the Hebrews and Jesus faced in the wilderness. Verse 3:1, "Did God really say, 'You must not eat from any tree in the garden'?" Verse 3:4, "You will not certainly die," the serpent said to the woman." Verse 3:5, "For God knows that when you eat from it your eyes will be opened, and you will be like God, knowing good and evil." These are some of Satan's oldest tricks, and yet, how many times does humanity fall like Adam and Eve every day?

As 1 John 2:16-17 tells us, "For everything in the world—the lust of the flesh, the lust of the eyes, and the pride of life—comes not from the Father but from the world." This verse warns that we cannot serve the world and God at the same time. It's a choice we must make daily. With faith, perseverance, and knowledge of God's Word, we can experience the ultimate victory in Christ.

Journal Questions

1. **Understanding the Warning of Unbelief:** In Hebrews 3:16, the author warns about the consequences of unbelief by comparing it to the Israelites' rebellion in the wilderness. Have you ever experienced a time when doubt or unbelief threatened your faith? How did you overcome it, and what steps can you take to strengthen your faith in difficult times?

2. **Learning from the Israelites' Failure:** The Israelites failed to enter God's rest because of their disobedience and lack of faith. How does this story serve as a cautionary example for Christians today? In what areas of your life might you be struggling with obedience or trust in God's promises?

3. **Perseverance in Faith:** Hebrews emphasizes the importance of perseverance. Can you recall a situation where you had to persevere in your faith despite challenges? What role did your trust in God play, and how can Caleb's example of faithfulness encourage you in your current walk with God?

4. **Resisting Temptation Like Jesus:** Both the Israelites and Jesus faced temptations in the wilderness. How do you handle temptations in your life, and how can Jesus' response to Satan's temptations (quoting Scripture) be a model for you to follow?

5. **The Role of Scripture in Strengthening Faith:** The narrative emphasizes the importance of God's Word in resisting temptation and staying faithful. How regularly do you engage with Scripture, and how can immersing yourself more in God's Word help you avoid the dangers of unbelief and spiritual complacency?

James 3:16

The letter of James is widely believed to be written by James, the brother of Jesus, and is addressed to Christians living in communities beyond the boundaries of Israel. The letter focuses on practical issues of Christian living, highlighting that faith without good deeds is dead. In James 2:18-19, he challenges the readers by pointing out that even demons believe in God, but their belief does not result in good works. This shows that faith alone, without action, is incomplete. James further explores the use of the tongue and how the way we speak reflects whether we are guided by heavenly wisdom or earthly wisdom.

In Chapter 3, James begins by warning people not to be too eager to become teachers. This isn't to discourage teaching, but rather to remind them of the heavy responsibility that comes with teaching God's Word. Teachers will be judged more strictly because they use the most dangerous part of the body: the tongue. The tongue can either build up or destroy. James calls controlling the tongue "perfect," meaning that it is an extremely difficult task that can only be mastered with wisdom and spiritual maturity.

James explains the power of the tongue, which is much greater than its size would suggest. He compares it to a bit in a horse's mouth, which guides the entire animal, or a small rudder that steers a large ship. Even though these are small objects, they have a huge influence, just as the tongue can affect the course of a person's life. A small spark can ignite a massive forest fire, and in the same way, the tongue can destroy relationships, reputations, and even faith if not controlled. This destructive potential, James warns, comes from the influence of Satan.

James 3:16 is part of a passage where James contrasts two kinds of wisdom: heavenly wisdom and earthly wisdom. He begins by asking, "Who is wise and understanding among you?" (3:13). He expects that true wisdom should be seen in a person's actions, not just their words. This connects back to James 2:20-24, where he states that Abraham was justified by his actions, not just by his faith. Heavenly wisdom is rooted in God's character and produces righteousness, peace, and unity. James describes heavenly wisdom, in verse 3:17, as "first of all pure; then peace-loving, considerate, submissive, full of mercy and good fruit, impartial and sincere". This wisdom encourages believers to act with humility and put others' needs before their own, just as Jesus did when He said in Matt 20:28, He came "not to be served, but to serve."

On the other hand, earthly wisdom is driven by jealousy, selfish ambition, and disorder. James says this wisdom is "earthly, unspiritual, and demonic" (3:15). Earthly wisdom leads to division and conflict, and its effects are destructive both personally and in communities. Proverbs 14:12 warns, "There is a way that appears to be right, but in the end, it leads to death." This shows how deceitful earthly wisdom can be, as it may seem appealing at first but leads to spiritual ruin.

Diotrephes, mentioned in 3 John 1:9-10, is an example of the warning in James 3:16, which says, "For where you have envy and selfish ambition, there you find disorder and every evil practice." Diotrephes, who was a leader in a local church, loved to put himself first and refused to welcome the apostles, including John. His ambition for power and his pride led to division within the church, much like what James describes. Instead of fostering unity, Diotrephes spread malicious gossip and even refused hospitality to other believers. His actions stand as a warning of how selfish ambition can bring disorder and harm to the church, aligning with Proverbs 16:18, "Pride goes before destruction, a haughty spirit before a fall."

In contrast, John exemplified the qualities of humility and love which James encourages. Paul gives similar advice in Philippians 2:3, saying, "Do nothing out of selfish ambition or vain conceit. Rather, in humility value others above yourselves." Diotrephes is a cautionary example of what happens when leaders let jealousy and ambition control them, leading to chaos and division within the community of believers, as James warns in 3:16.

James stresses that believers must actively resist worldly temptations and choose heavenly wisdom. This means taking responsibility for their spiritual growth, cultivating humility, and rejecting jealousy and selfish ambitions. In Philippians 2:3-4, Paul instructs believers to foster unity and harmony by practicing humility, grace, and forgiveness, which creates a Christ-centered community. This also requires reflecting on one's motives, ensuring that actions are driven by love and service to others, rather than by personal gain or selfish desires.

James' emphasis on faith accompanied by good works is echoed in Colossians 3:17, where he says, "And whatever you do, whether in word or deed, do it all in the name of the Lord Jesus, giving thanks to God the Father through him." By seeking and embracing heavenly wisdom, believers are empowered to navigate the challenges of life with grace, integrity, and the wisdom that comes from God. This not only strengthens personal faith but also builds up the entire Christian community, reflecting the transformative power of Christ.

Journal Questions

1. **The Destructive Power of Jealousy and Ambition:** James 3:16 warns that jealousy and selfish ambition lead to disorder and evil practices. Can you recall a time when jealousy or selfish ambition impacted your relationships or actions? How did it affect you and others, and what steps can you take to guard your heart against these attitudes in the future?

2. **Choosing Heavenly Wisdom Over Earthly Wisdom:** James contrasts heavenly wisdom, which promotes peace and righteousness, with earthly wisdom, which leads to conflict and strife. In what areas of your life are you tempted to rely on earthly wisdom? How can you actively pursue godly wisdom in those situations, and what changes would it bring to your relationships?
3. **The Power of the Tongue:** James highlights how the tongue can either bring life or destruction. Reflect on how your words have impacted those around you. Are there areas where your speech has caused harm or division? What can you do to ensure that your words align with heavenly wisdom and encourage unity and peace?
4. **Guarding Against Selfish Desires:** James teaches that selfish ambition leads to disorder. Have you ever found yourself pursuing something out of selfish ambition rather than out of love or service to others? How can you realign your motivations to reflect humility and the interests of others above your own?
5. **Cultivating a Christ-like Community:** James encourages believers to foster unity through humility and selflessness. How are you contributing to the unity and peace of your community—whether at church, work, or home? What steps can you take to foster a Christ-like environment where heavenly wisdom, rather than selfish ambition, prevails?

21

1 Peter 3:16

1 Peter is believed to be written by the Apostle Peter, one of Jesus' closest disciples and a leader of the early church in Jerusalem. The letter was written to encourage Christians to remain strong in their faith, even when facing hostility or persecution. Peter's message is one of hope, urging believers to follow Christ's example when they are misunderstood or mistreated by the world. He also stresses the importance of keeping a clear conscience and being ready to explain and defend their faith with gentleness and respect. In 1 Peter, there is a lot of wisdom and practical advice for Christian living in difficult times.

Peter begins the letter by praising God, reminding believers of the new life they have received through Jesus. 1 Peter 1:4 speaks of an "inheritance that can never perish, spoil, or fade," showing that believers can stand firm in their faith because they know their ultimate future is secure in God. This is a blessing that those who do not believe in Christ do not have, as they face the uncertainties of life without hope for tomorrow.

In Chapter Two, Peter compares believers to stones in a "spiritual house," with Jesus as the cornerstone. This image is similar to Paul's teaching in 1 Corinthians 12, where he describes believers as different parts of the body of Christ, all working together. Both pictures encourage believers, reminding them that even in times of personal suffering or hostility, they are part of a united community of faith that has survived for over two thousand years.

In Chapter Three, Peter teaches believers how to live in a world that is often hostile to their faith. He encourages unity, humility, and love in response to insults and evil treatment. Instead of repaying evil with evil, Peter calls Christians to act from a heart that trusts in God's care, following the example of Jesus, who showed love even to His enemies. This mirrors Jesus' teaching from the Sermon on the Mount, Matthew 5:44, where He tells His followers to "love your enemies and pray for those who persecute you." Peter emphasizes that Christians must reflect God's goodness, not the brokenness of the world.

Peter also encourages believers to maintain a "clear conscience" in the face of hostility. A clear conscience means that their actions align with their faith, and that they can be bold in sharing their hope in Christ. He reminds them to do so with gentleness and respect, allowing their lives to show the difference that Christ has made.

Maintaining a clear conscience also brings blessings from God. Although doing what is right should not usually result in harm, Peter acknowledges that sometimes Christians will suffer for their faith. He tells believers not to be afraid of suffering but to honor Christ as Lord in their hearts. This is echoed in Isaiah 8:13, where it says, "The Lord Almighty is the one you are to regard as holy; he is the one you are to fear." This kind of deep trust in Jesus should cause others to notice the hope in believers' lives and ask about it, giving Christians the opportunity to share their faith.

Stephen, the first Christian martyr, exemplifies 1 Peter 3:16. Stephen was one of seven chosen to serve the early church, known for being full of faith and the Holy Spirit. Even when he was falsely accused of blasphemy by certain Jewish leaders, Stephen remained calm and confident in his faith. His face was described as shining "like the face of an angel" (Acts 6:15), showing that he had a clear conscience before God and man.

When brought before the Sanhedrin, Stephen boldly defended his faith by recounting Israel's history and accusing the religious leaders of rejecting God's truth. His courage reflected the words of Isaiah 50:7, "Because the Sovereign Lord helps me, I will not be disgraced." Even as Stephen was being stoned to death, he prayed for those who were killing him, asking God to forgive them (Acts 7:60). This act of grace and forgiveness mirrors the spirit of 1 Peter 3:16, showing how a clear conscience and a Christ-like response to persecution brings honor to God and leaves those who accuse in shame.

1 Peter 3:16 reminds believers to stand firm in their faith and be ready to share the hope they have in Christ with integrity and gentleness. To do this, Christians need to be consistent in their spiritual disciplines—studying and abiding in God's Word, praying often, and living each day with the desire to reflect Christ's love to everyone they meet. This preparation helps believers remain steadfast and bold, even in the face of persecution, and allows them to be effective witnesses for Christ in a world that often opposes their faith.

Journal Questions

1. **Maintaining a Clear Conscience:** 1 Peter 3:16 emphasizes the importance of living with a clear conscience, even when facing hostility. Are there any areas in your life where you feel your actions or words are not aligned with your faith? How can you bring these areas into alignment with Christ's example?
2. **Responding with Gentleness and Respect:** When sharing your faith or responding to opposition, how do you typically react? Do you respond with gentleness and respect as Peter instructs, or do you find yourself becoming defensive or frustrated? How can you improve in this area?
3. **Boldness in Sharing Your Faith:** Peter encourages believers to be ready to share the reason for their hope in Christ. Have you ever felt hesitant or afraid to share your faith? What can you do to grow in boldness while still speaking with love and humility?

4. **Following Christ's Example in Suffering:** 1 Peter 3:16 reminds us that even when we suffer for doing good, we can follow Christ's example. How do you typically respond to unfair treatment or persecution? What can you learn from Christ's and Stephen's example of responding to mistreatment with grace?

5. **Preparing to Defend Your Faith:** Peter urges believers to be prepared to defend their faith. How often do you study Scripture and engage in practices that deepen your understanding of your faith? What steps can you take to ensure you are spiritually prepared to answer others about the hope you have in Christ?

22

2 Peter 3:16

Many early Christians never met Jesus Christ in person or heard Him speak. Their knowledge of Him came from preachers known as apostles and their companions. Luke, one of these early Christians, decided to write a sequel to the Gospels, known as the Acts of the Apostles. This book records how the Holy Spirit worked to spread the message of Jesus from Jerusalem to the rest of the world. Two main figures in Acts are Peter and Paul. Both went on many missionary journeys, sharing the gospel as far as they could until their lives came to an end.

Peter wrote 2 Peter toward the end of his life. In 2 Peter 1:13-14, he hints that he knows his time is near: "I think it is right to refresh your memory...because I know that I will soon put [my body] aside, as our Lord Jesus Christ has made clear to me." True to Peter's direct and practical personality, this letter warns early Christians about false teachings and moral compromise. He clearly states his purpose in 2 Peter 3:1-2, reminding them to think clearly and recall the teachings of the prophets and the commands of Jesus.

2 Peter 3:16 is found in the part of the letter that addresses concerns about the end times, warning against worldly corruption and false teachers. As Peter's life was nearing its end, his letter focused on these key issues, urging the church not to be led astray by those who distort the truth. He acknowledges that Paul's letters can be hard to

understand but urges readers to trust in the authority and reliability of all Scripture.

The word "Scripture" appears many times in the New Testament, often referring to the Old Testament. However, Peter gives the same authority to the apostles' letters, including Paul's and his own. This shows the unity of Scripture and highlights the need to study the Bible as a whole, understanding its consistent message of salvation and godly living.

2 Peter 3:16 stresses the importance of interpreting Scripture correctly. Misunderstanding or twisting its message can lead to confusion or even serious errors in belief. Peter warns that some people distort Scripture, highlighting the danger of false teaching in the church. Like the Bereans in Acts 17, who "examined the Scriptures every day to see if what Paul said was true," Christians must build a solid foundation of biblical knowledge to avoid being misled.

Peter's message also points to the need for spiritual growth. Those who are spiritually immature are more vulnerable to false teachings. Paul emphasizes the benefits of growth in Ephesians 4:14-15: "Then we will no longer be infants, tossed back and forth by the waves... Instead, speaking the truth in love, we will grow to become the mature body of Christ." Spiritual growth helps believers discern truth from error, as reinforced in 2 Timothy 3:16, which says that "all Scripture is God-breathed."

Philip the Evangelist embodies the message of 2 Peter 3:16. In Acts 8:26-40, Philip encounters an Ethiopian eunuch reading the book of Isaiah but struggling to understand it. Philip explains how Isaiah's prophecy points to Jesus, helping the eunuch understand the gospel and leading him to faith and baptism. This story shows the importance of correctly understanding Scripture, just as Peter emphasizes.

Philip's life illustrates the wisdom in Proverbs 4:7, which says, "The beginning of wisdom is this: Get wisdom. Though it cost all you have, get understanding." Through proper guidance, the eunuch gained life-changing understanding, just as we are called to seek true understanding of Scripture rather than twisting it to fit personal views.

Believers must approach the Bible with humility, recognizing that everyone can grow and learn. We need to allow God's Word to shape our thinking and actions. Developing discernment and testing everything against Scripture will help us avoid false teachings. Committing to lifelong study and growing in our understanding of the Bible will deepen our relationship with God and strengthen our faith.

Journal Questions

1. **The Role of Scripture in Spiritual Growth:** 2 Peter 3:16 warns against misinterpreting Scripture and encourages spiritual growth through proper understanding. Have you encountered any difficult passages in the Bible that you struggled to understand? How can you commit to deeper study and seek guidance from mature believers to gain better understanding?
2. **Guarding Against False Teachings:** Peter warns about the dangers of false teachers distorting the truth. How do you discern between true and false teachings in your spiritual journey? What steps can you take to develop stronger discernment in your faith?
3. **The Importance of Unity in Scripture:** Peter places Paul's letters on the same level as the Old Testament Scripture, affirming their authority. How do you view the unity of Scripture from both the Old and New Testaments? In what ways can you deepen your appreciation for the Bible as a whole, seeing the consistent message of salvation throughout?
4. **Responding to Spiritual Immaturity:** 2 Peter 3:16 highlights the vulnerability of those who are "unstable" and untaught in the faith. How can you actively pursue spiritual maturity to ensure you are not easily led astray by false teachings? How does your daily time in the Word reflect a commitment to growing in Christ?

5. **The Humility of Seeking Understanding:** Philip helped the Ethiopian eunuch understand Scripture, demonstrating the value of guidance. Have you ever sought help from others to understand a difficult part of the Bible? How can seeking wisdom and humility in studying Scripture lead to deeper spiritual transformation in your life?

23

1 John 3:16

In his first letter, John addresses the dangers of false teachings, which were troubling the early Christian community, similar to the challenges Paul and Peter encountered. John's writing emphasizes living rightly, following God's commands, and having confidence in salvation through Christ alone. He uses familiar language and imagery from his Gospel, focusing on the concept of "beginning."

In his Gospel, John starts with "In the beginning" to show that Jesus is eternal, the Word of God, and the light that overcomes darkness (John 1:1-5). In 1 John 1:1, he writes, "from the beginning," to affirm that Jesus truly became human and walked among them, saying, "we have seen with our eyes, which we have looked at and our hands have touched." His Gospel emphasizes Jesus' divinity, while this letter reassures the readers of His humanity, addressing those who thought Jesus was only divine.

In his Gospel, John describes Jesus as the light shining in the darkness, which the darkness cannot overcome. In 1 John, he connects Jesus' light to His sinlessness, which allows us to bring our sins to Him to be made pure in His light. John makes it clear that if we claim to be in the light, it must be through faith and fellowship with Jesus. There is no "in-between" because Jesus, as the divine Word, took on humanity to bring renewal to all people. This is a foundational truth of the faith.

In 1 John 3:16, John presents a simple but powerful message: God's love is shown through Jesus' ultimate sacrifice. When people truly understand Jesus and His mission, they'll see that God's nature is self-giving love. The call to "love one another" reflects God's nature, asking believers to share in His love. In Matthew 22:37-40, Jesus perfectly explained this: "Love the Lord your God with all your heart…soul…mind…[and] love your neighbor as yourself." This is the heart of God's message and is shown clearly through Jesus' sacrifice.

John urges believers to reflect Christ's sacrificial love in their lives, prioritizing others' well-being and sometimes making personal sacrifices. In 1 John 3:16, he emphasizes what is taught in John 15:13, "Greater love has no one than this: to lay down one's life for one's friends." This call to selfless love extends beyond friends to family, coworkers, neighbors, and fellow believers. This sacrificial love strengthens bonds within the church, building a community where everyone feels supported and valued. It also transcends social and cultural divisions. Paul highlights this unity in Galatians 3:28: "You are all one in Christ Jesus." This diverse yet united community reflects Christ's love and creates a powerful witness to the world.

Joseph of Arimathea embodies the message of 1 John 3:16: "This is how we know what love is: Jesus Christ laid down his life for us." Joseph's actions after Jesus' death show courageous, self-sacrificial love. Though he was a wealthy member of the Jewish council and a follower of Jesus, he risked his reputation and standing to ensure Jesus received a proper burial. When Jesus' other followers fled, Joseph boldly approached Pilate to request Jesus' body, demonstrating loyalty and respect (Mark 15:43). By offering his own tomb, Joseph sacrificed not only personal gain but also faced repercussions from the council and community.

Joseph's actions align with Proverbs 21:21, which states, "Whoever pursues righteousness and love finds life, prosperity, and honor." Although he acted quietly, his loyalty and love for Jesus shines through his actions, putting aside his comfort to care for Jesus in His time of need. Joseph's example demonstrates the selfless devotion 1 John 3:16 calls believers to embody.

At the center of Christianity is God's love for humanity, shown in the sacrifice of His Son, which reconciles us to Him. John states, "This is love: not that we loved God, but that he loved us and sent his Son as an atoning sacrifice for our sins." Love is active, not passive shapes character, transforms lives, and unites believers. This love calls Christians to do more than speak words of kindness; it compels them to act, putting others' needs before their own. Whether through giving time, resources, or support, believers are called to love as God loves with a transformative power that reflects His character and invites others to experience His grace. This love is the foundation of the Christian life and the path to unity, strength, and spiritual growth within the community of faith.

Journal Questions

1. **Understanding Sacrificial Love:** In 1 John 3:16, we see that Jesus' sacrificial love is the ultimate example for us. Have you encountered a time when showing love required personal sacrifice? How did it impact your relationship with others, and how might it have helped others see Christ's love through you?
2. **Living in the Light:** John emphasizes that walking in the light means living with faith in Jesus and fellowship with others. Are there areas of your life where you feel challenged to live fully in the light? How can you invite Jesus to help you strengthen those areas and reflect His purity and love?
3. **Moving Beyond Words to Action:** John calls believers to show love not just with words but through selfless actions. How might you demonstrate Christ-like love this week? Are there people in your life, such as family, friends, and coworkers who could benefit from acts of kindness or support?
4. **Unity and Community in Christ:** Sacrificial love helps build a strong, united community. Reflect on your relationships

within your faith community. How are you actively contributing to unity and support within this group? What steps can you take to embrace a more inclusive, Christ-centered community?

5. **Growing in Humility and Selflessness:** Joseph of Arimathea exemplified humility and sacrifice by caring for Jesus despite potential risks. Are there moments when humility might have helped you prioritize others' needs over your own? How can you follow Joseph's example, using your resources or position to serve others and honor Christ?

24

2 John

The second letter of John, though brief, is rich with encouragement for the early church and for us today. Despite its short length, this letter emphasizes the need for Christians to hold tightly to both truth and love. John highlights that truth and love must work together. Love without truth can drift into error, while truth without love can become harsh. In all of John's writings, these two qualities are inseparable and are the best defense against attacks from the enemy.

The letter is addressed to "the lady chosen by God and to her children." Scholars debate whether this refers to a specific woman and her family or if it's a metaphor for a local church and its members. In the early church, many house churches met in people's homes, and women often played important roles as hosts. John's gospel emphasizes the role of women, too, showing their significance in the ministry of Jesus and in the spread of the faith.

For instance, in John 4, Jesus has a conversation with the Samaritan woman, leading to her conversion and the conversion of many others. Martha, in John 11, makes a powerful confession of faith, declaring Jesus as the Messiah. Mary, her sister, anoints Jesus before His burial, honoring Him in a significant way. At the crucifixion His mother, Mary, and other women were witnesses. Finally, Mary Magdeline is the first to see the empty tomb and speak to the resurrected Jesus. These examples show that John viewed women as essential to the ministry and growth of the early church.

Regardless of the exact identity of "the lady," John's message is clear: Christians must love one another and hold firmly to the truth of Jesus' teachings. He encourages believers to "walk in truth" by obeying God's commands and staying true to the gospel, even in the face of opposition. This theme of resisting false teachings was common among the early church leaders as they wrote to protect the young church.

John also warns, in verse 10, against welcoming false teachers, those who oppose Christ's divinity and spread deception. He advises, "do not take [them] into your house or welcome them." This instruction applies specifically to those actively spreading false doctrines, not to ordinary non-believers. We are still called to be welcoming and to share God's Word with everyone, so that all might come to know Him. However, believers are to exercise discernment when it comes to those who distort God's truth.

In a world filled with shifting morals and values, John's words are highly relevant. He describes opponents of the gospel as doing "wicked work" in verse 11, whether they realize who the source of this destruction is or not. Believers are encouraged to be both loving and discerning, extending compassion even to those who may be deceived. Matthew 5:44 states that Jesus' call to "love your enemies and pray for those who persecute you" remains essential to our faith.

Priscilla, an early Christian leader, exemplifies the message of 2 John. Along with her husband, Aquila, Priscilla taught others about Christ and was a key figure in the early church. When Apollos, an eloquent preacher, arrived in Ephesus with an incomplete understanding of the gospel, Priscilla and Aquila took him aside, "explaining the way of God more accurately" (Acts 18:26). Their approach reflected both love and commitment to truth, providing guidance without harshness.

Priscilla's actions align with Proverbs 3:3, "Let love and faithfulness never leave you; bind them around your neck, write them on the tablet of your heart." Her commitment to both love and truth is a model of John's message in 2 John. She balanced love with discernment, teaching Apollos and helping him grow in his ministry.

The message of 2 John reminds believers that truth and love are essential for a strong Christian life. Jesus prayed, "Sanctify them by the truth; your word is truth" (John 17:17). This letter is also a call to discernment, echoing Paul's words to "test them all; hold on to what is good, reject every kind of evil" (1 Thessalonians 5:21-22). In a world where false teachings still exist, believers must hold everything up to Scripture as their standard.

By living out the message of 2 John, Christians reflect God's character and build strong, healthy relationships within the church. This unity within the body of Christ serves as a powerful witness to the world, showing that a life grounded in truth and love is transformative and reflects the true nature of God.

Journal Questions

1. **Balancing Truth and Love:** 2 John emphasizes the importance of balancing truth and love in our faith. Do you find it easier to lean toward one over the other? How can you grow in both areas to ensure you live with both compassion and conviction in your relationships?
2. **Responding to False Teachings:** John warns against welcoming those who spread false teachings. Have you encountered situations where you felt challenged by ideas or beliefs contrary to biblical teachings? How do you discern truth, and how can you strengthen your understanding of Scripture to respond with wisdom and grace?
3. **Hospitality with Discernment:** John encourages believers to be hospitable but warns against supporting those who spread false beliefs. How can you show hospitality and kindness to others while staying true to your beliefs? What boundaries can you set to uphold your faith without compromising love?

4. **Living as a Witness to the Truth:** John calls believers to "walk in truth" as a way of life. How does this commitment to truth influence your daily actions and decisions? In what areas of your life can you better reflect Christ's truth and love to those around you?
5. **Learning from Faithful Examples:** Priscilla, as a model of love and truth, taught others about Christ with kindness and accuracy. Who are some people in your life or in Scripture that have demonstrated a balanced walk of truth and love? How can their example inspire you to live out your faith more fully?

25

3 John

3 John is the shortest book in the New Testament, and while John doesn't mention Jesus directly, he emphasizes key traits like love and truth, which are deeply associated with Jesus. Even though this letter is brief, John clearly contrasts living with truth and hospitality versus living with pride and hostility. These two traits—truth and hospitality—are essential behaviors that all Christians should strive to model.

John uses the word "truth" five times in just fourteen verses, showing how important it is to live by biblical truth and stay true to it, even when it's hard. By lifting up Gaius as an example, John praises him as a person who lives by the truth, which reflects his sincere faith and impacts those around him. Psalm 119:160 reinforces this idea, saying, "All your words are true."

Throughout his letters, John links truth with love repeatedly. Christians are called to love everyone (Galatians 6:10), both the righteous and the unrighteous (Matthew 5:43-48), as Jesus loves us. In Gaius, John shows how love and truth go hand in hand and how love produces hospitality. On the other hand, Diotrephes, who lacks love and hospitality, reflects a way of living that does not reveal God.

Hospitality was a core value in Jewish culture and many other ancient societies. We see examples of hospitality in the Old Testament, like Melchizedek hosting Abraham (Genesis 14:18), and in the New Testament, with people like Zaccheus welcoming Jesus (John 4:40).

Hospitality is more than a social custom for Christians; it's a duty. Today, missionaries visiting churches often stay with local church members instead of hotels, which reflects the community spirit John praises in Gaius.

Paul calls hospitality an act of love in Romans 12:13, "Share with the Lord's people who are in need. Practice hospitality." Hebrews 13:2 adds, "Do not forget to show hospitality to strangers, for by so doing some people have shown hospitality to angels without knowing it." In 3 John, Gaius is commended for his generosity toward traveling missionaries, showing the importance of supporting believers who are actively serving the Lord.

The phrase, "It was for the sake of the Name that they went out" (3 John 7) serves as a reminder to support others in the name of God Himself. Missionaries and teachers of the gospel, in John's time and today, deserve to be loved, welcomed, and supported in truth and hospitality as they carry out Christ's mission.

Then there is Diotrephes. His exact role in the church isn't fully known, but he's described as someone who "loves to be first," showing his pride and lack of respect for John and other leaders. This pride, one of the Bible's most dangerous sins because it comes from the heart and leads people to forget God and become unfaithful and ungrateful. Proverbs 16:18 warns, "Pride goes before destruction, a haughty spirit before a fall."

Pride has been a downfall for many in the Bible, from Eve to kings like Absalom and Nebuchadnezzar. In the New Testament, pride caused the mother of James and John to ask that her sons sit beside Jesus in His kingdom, stirring anger among the other disciples. Jesus turned this prideful moment into a lesson on humility and servanthood.

Cornelius, a Roman centurion, exemplifies the message of 3 John by showing truth, hospitality, and a supportive spirit toward the gospel. Even before hearing the gospel, Cornelius is described as "devout and God-fearing" (Acts 10:2), and he generously gave to those in need. When he received a vision to call for Peter, he eagerly gathered his household to listen. Cornelius' hospitality and openness to the truth align with Gaius' faithful spirit in 3 John.

As Peter preached, Cornelius and his household were filled with the Holy Spirit, marking the first Gentile conversions, and bridging Jewish and Gentile believers. Cornelius' faithfulness and hospitality show how welcoming hearts can lead to great spiritual growth and unity.

3 John calls modern believers to live with truth and hospitality, modeling the generosity of Gaius rather than the pride of Diotrephes. John's praise of Gaius urges us to live with hospitality as an expression of God's love, encouraging and supporting others in the faith, especially those in ministry. The letter contrasts Gaius' genuine faith with Diotrephes' pride, showing us how living in the truth of God's Word makes it possible to act in love and humility.

Journal Questions

1. **Living in Truth:** Gaius is commended for his commitment to walking in truth. Are there areas in your life where you feel called to live more truthfully according to God's Word? How can you ensure that your faith is grounded in biblical truth, especially when faced with challenges?
2. **Showing Hospitality:** Gaius demonstrates a welcoming heart by supporting fellow believers. How might you practice hospitality and generosity towards others in your life, especially those in the ministry, or those in need? What specific actions can you take to extend Christ-like kindness and support?
3. **Guarding Against Pride:** Diotrephes allowed pride to impact his actions and relationships. How can you guard your heart against pride and instead serve others humbly? Are there any situations where pride might be keeping you from truly serving God and others?
4. **Supporting Mission Work:** John emphasizes the importance of supporting those who share the gospel. How can you actively

support those in the ministry, either locally or globally? Are there ways you can contribute to the spread of the gospel through prayer, financial support, or personal involvement?
5. **Balancing Truth and Love:** John highlights that truth and love must go hand in hand. In what ways can you uphold God's truth while showing love to others? How can you ensure that your actions reflect both truth and compassion in your daily interactions with those around you?

26

Jude

Jude begins his letter with a clear and urgent tone, letting his readers know that although he had planned to write about the joy of salvation, a pressing issue within the church has forced him to shift his focus. He now has to confront the threat of false teachers who have infiltrated the Christian community, preaching a distorted gospel and twisting Scripture for their own purposes. These false teachers not only deny the authority of Jesus but also encourage ungodly living, posing a real danger to the faith of those in the church. Jude's response to this situation is passionate and direct, drawing on vivid examples from the Old Testament to underscore his warning.

The urgency of Jude's message can be broken down into two main themes that emerge in verses 3 and 4. In verse 3, Jude calls on the church to "contend for the faith." This isn't a gentle reminder but a strong call to action against the serious challenge posed by these false teachings. Jude wants the believers to act quickly and decisively, recognizing that the faith they hold is under attack. He knows that if they do not address the issue immediately, it could weaken the church and harm the unity of the congregation. To reinforce the seriousness of this struggle, Jude reminds his readers of the dire consequences of letting ungodly influences persist, framing his message as a spiritual battle with eternal consequences.

Before Jude provides a kind of "handbook" on discipleship in verses 17-23, he establishes a foundation by emphasizing the need for believers to be aware of the threat around them and prepared to act. He encourages them to remain vigilant and persevere through the challenges posed by these false teachers. In verses 17-23, he provides specific instructions on how they should strengthen themselves and each other. Jude uses memorable phrases like "remember" the apostles, "keep" themselves in God's love, "build" up their faith, and "pray in the Holy Spirit." Jude is guiding them on how to guard their faith actively. He also stresses showing mercy to those who are doubting or struggling, saying, "save others by snatching them from the fire." His words are a reminder of the high stakes involved in this spiritual battle, urging believers to stay focused on preserving both their faith and the faith of others within the community.

In verse 4, Jude shifts his focus to the specific threat that has come into the congregation, namely individuals who "pervert the grace of our God" and live immorally. To illustrate the consequences of such behavior, he uses three examples of Old Testament in verses 5-7. Jude reminds them of the unfaithfulness of the Israelites in the wilderness, which led to their punishment; of certain rebellious angels who abandoned their position and were cast into darkness; and of the sinful practices in Sodom and Gomorrah, which resulted in destruction by fire. Each example was familiar to his audience, underscoring that God has always responded to rebellion with divine judgment. Jude's message is that the same principles of accountability and judgment apply to the church's current situation: just as God judged disobedience in the past, He will judge those who continue to lead others astray.

Jude then strengthens his warning by using three additional examples—Cain, Balaam, and Korah—in verses 11-13. Cain's jealousy led him to murder his brother Abel, while Balaam's greed caused him to lead Israel into sin for personal gain. Korah's pride drove him to challenge the authority of Moses, leading to his destruction. These examples of rebellion, greed, and pride serve as a stark reminder of the destructive consequences that come from defying God's commands. Jude uses these examples to show that such behaviors aren't just harmless mistakes but serious offenses that God cannot overlook. He warns that those who follow the paths of Cain, Balaam, and Korah are destined for "blackest darkness," emphasizing the severity of their actions.

Jude's letter calls believers to recognize this spiritual battle as a matter of life and death. False teachings and ungodly influences can disrupt not only individuals but the entire church. His message is that ignoring these issues or allowing them to continue unchecked is not an option. Jude's words remain deeply relevant to today's church, as false teachings and moral compromises continue to threaten Christian communities around the world. Just as the early church was called to stand firm in the face of deception, so too are believers today. Jude's letter serves as a reminder that the integrity of the gospel should never be compromised for the sake of fitting in with cultural trends or avoiding conflict.

Jude's call to contend for the faith is much more than simply confronting false teachings. It's also about nurturing and strengthening believers' relationships with God. Jude urges the church to stay close to God through prayer, worship, and obedience, laying out a clear path for spiritual growth in verses 17-23. His advice to "build" one another up, "pray in the Holy Spirit," and "keep in God's love" are essential steps for maintaining a strong faith. Jude encourages believers to show mercy to those who doubt and to be compassionate while remaining cautious of those who are unrepentant in their sin. By focusing on spiritual growth and staying grounded in the truth, believers can protect themselves from falling prey to falsehoods.

Jude's message is brought to life through the example of Phinehas, the grandson of Aaron. During the Israelites' journey in the wilderness, many people began to worship false gods and fall into immoral behavior with the Moabites. This rebellion was severe enough that a plague broke out among the Israelites. In the midst of this turmoil, an Israelite man openly defied God's commands by bringing a Midianite woman into the camp, directly challenging God's holiness. Phinehas, filled with zeal for God's honor, took swift action to stop the sin and protect the community. His boldness halted the plague and preserved Israel from further destruction (Numbers 25:6-8). God praised Phinehas, saying, "He was as zealous as I am for my honor among them, so that in my zeal I did not put an end to them" (Numbers 25:11). Phinehas's dedication to protecting God's honor and his willingness to act without hesitation serve as powerful examples of the kind of zeal Jude urges believers to embody.

Jude's message is a call for all believers to actively defend their faith, remain grounded in God's truth, and stay vigilant against deception. His examples from the Old Testament show that God takes rebellion and disobedience seriously, and that believers are called to uphold the truth with both courage and compassion. Jude reminds us that we are accountable to God, and that He expects us to live lives of integrity and faithfulness. The epistle serves as a powerful reminder that the church must stay strong in its commitment to the gospel, guarding against anything that distorts the message of salvation.

Journal Questions

1. **Contending for the Faith:** Jude urges believers to "contend for the faith" in the face of false teachings. Are there specific areas where you feel challenged in defending your faith today? How can you strengthen your understanding of Scripture to confidently stand against these challenges?
2. **Learning from Past Warnings:** Jude uses examples from the Old Testament, like the Israelites in the wilderness, Sodom, and Gomorrah, to remind us of the consequences of disobedience. How do these examples inspire you to remain obedient to God's Word? Are there particular lessons from these stories that resonate with your own spiritual journey?
3. **Embracing Spiritual Growth:** In verses 17-23, Jude emphasizes building each other up and staying strong in faith. How can you practice "building up" your faith and the faith of others?

Are there specific ways you feel called to encourage others in your Christian community?

4. **Living with Zeal like Phinehas:** Jude calls believers to be vigilant in their commitment to holiness, just as Phinehas zealously defended God's honor. Are there areas in your life where you feel called to take a stronger stand for God's truth and holiness? How might you, like Phinehas, take action that honors God?

5. **Showing Mercy with Discernment:** Jude encourages believers to "be merciful to those who doubt" but also to "show mercy, mixed with fear." How do you balance compassion with discernment when approaching those who may have fallen away or are struggling in their faith? How can you help others see the importance of both grace and truth in their walk with God?

27

Revelation 3:16

Laodicea is the last of the seven churches Jesus addresses directly, but this is not a happy conclusion to the letters. Laodicea was a very wealthy city, positioned at the crossroads of several trade routes. It was so wealthy, in fact, that when an earthquake nearly destroyed it in 60 C.E., the city refused any help from the Roman Empire, choosing instead to rebuild with its own resources. This self-reliant attitude symbolized the church's spiritual condition.

Laodicea's location also shaped Jesus' message. Sitting on a high plateau with no natural springs nearby, the city had to bring in water from a distance through stone aqueducts. The cold springs from Colossae, ten miles to the east, and the hot springs from Hierapolis, six miles to the north, provided stark contrasts to Laodicea's lukewarm water by the time it reached the city. The minerals made the water taste bitter, and people would often spit it out. Jesus uses this familiar experience to highlight the spiritual complacency of the Laodicean church.

When Jesus describes the church as "lukewarm," He isn't saying they should be "on fire" for ministry or entirely inactive. Instead, He points out how their half-hearted faith has become ineffective. It's as if He's telling them, "Make up your mind—choose either to be completely committed or not at all!" The Laodicean church was comfortable and self-sufficient, relying more on their wealth than on a true relationship with Jesus. They thought they didn't need anything, yet

Jesus saw their true spiritual state as lacking in devotion and righteousness. James reminds us of the need for true faith with deeds: "What good is it...if someone claims to have faith but has no deeds? Can such faith save them?" (James 2:14).

This warning applies to churches today, too. When things are going well—attendance is up, and funds are flowing in—it's easy to become self-reliant. But relying on our own resources instead of the Holy Spirit's power leads to spiritual complacency. In this state of comfort and success, we risk losing the sense of our deep need for Jesus in every area of life.

Despite the church's lukewarm state, Jesus' love for His church is so strong that He extends an invitation: "Here I am! Open the door, and we can worship together." His call is not just for the whole church but for each person. This open invitation reminds us that Jesus left the ninety-nine to find the one lost sheep. Even in times of prosperity, we are warned not to let our faith cool or our worship become lukewarm.

King Amaziah's story in the Old Testament illustrates Revelation 3:16: "Because you are lukewarm—neither hot nor cold—I am about to spit you out of my mouth." King Amaziah of Judah is an example of half-hearted devotion that leads to downfall. Amaziah began his reign with some obedience to God, yet 2 Chronicles 25:2 says, "He did what was right in the eyes of the Lord, but not wholeheartedly." His devotion was incomplete. After a victory over the Edomites, Amaziah chose to worship their idols, directly defying the God who had given him victory (2 Chronicles 25:14). When warned by a prophet, Amaziah ignored him, allowing pride to guide him instead of true loyalty to God.

Amaziah's lukewarm devotion led to disastrous choices, like his failed war with Israel. He neither fully embraced God's ways nor fully abandoned them, demonstrating the danger of half-heartedness that Revelation 3:16 warns against. His story echoes Elijah's challenge to Israel: "How long will you waver between two opinions? If the Lord is God, follow him; but if Baal is God, follow him" (1 Kings 18:21).

Amaziah's failure to commit wholeheartedly is a cautionary tale about the dangers of a divided heart.

Revelation 3:16 calls Christians to take their faith seriously, rejecting lukewarm attitudes. A half-hearted relationship with Jesus devalues His divinity and His teachings. This warning also underscores the reality of divine judgment for spiritual indifference. Believers are encouraged to nurture their faith actively through spiritual practices like prayer, study, worship, and serving others. These actions foster intimacy with God and connection with other believers.

The letter to Laodicea opens with, "These are the words of the Amen, the faithful and true witness." Jesus is the ultimate "Amen," affirming the truth of God's Word. In worship services, saying "Amen" is a way to agree with the truth being proclaimed. The entire Bible ends with "Amen" in Revelation 22:21, underscoring the reliability and finality of God's message through Jesus. As this message to Laodicea is the final lesson in this book, I, the author, say to you, the reader, "Amen!"

Journal Questions

1. **Examining Self-Sufficiency:** The Laodicean church relied on its own wealth rather than on God. Are there areas in your life where you may be relying more on personal resources or achievements than on your faith in Jesus? How can you shift toward greater dependence on God?
2. **Reflecting on Spiritual Temperature:** Jesus used the imagery of lukewarm water to illustrate Laodicea's spiritual state. Would you describe your faith as "hot," "cold," or "lukewarm"? What changes can you make to reignite your passion for Christ if it has faded?
3. **Receiving Jesus' Invitation:** Despite their complacency, Jesus called the Laodiceans to open the door to renewed fellowship with Him. How can you respond to Jesus' invitation to deeper

relationship in your life? What might you need to let go of to welcome Him fully?

4. **Learning from King Amaziah's Example:** King Amaziah started strong but fell due to half-hearted devotion. In what ways can his story encourage you to seek wholehearted commitment to God? Are there any "idols" or distractions in your life that might weaken your relationship with Him?

5. **Embracing the Call to Wholehearted Faith:** Revelation 3:16 challenges believers to avoid lukewarm faith. How does this verse encourage you to examine the depth of your commitment to Christ? What practical steps can you take to keep your faith vibrant and actively engaged in serving God and others?

Section Two

"The Bible is not the light of the world, it is the light of the Church. But the world does not read the Bible, the world reads Chris- tians! 'You are the light of the world.'"

Charles Spurgeon

"The Word of God well understood and religiously obeyed is the shortest route to spiritual perfection."

A.W. Tozer

Discussion Questions

Chapter 1

1. Why do you think Jesus chose to be baptized, even though He was without sin? What does this reveal about His character and mission?
2. John initially resisted baptizing Jesus, saying he was unworthy. Have you ever felt unworthy to serve God in some way? How did you overcome that feeling?
3. The heavens opening and the Spirit descending as a dove is a profound moment in Matthew 3:16. What does this imagery suggest about the Holy Spirit's role in Jesus's ministry and in our lives today?
4. God's voice declares Jesus as His beloved Son, affirming His identity and mission. How does knowing you are loved and chosen by God impact your faith and daily life?
5. Jesus's baptism is a moment of humility and obedience. How can we model humility and obedience in our faith journey?
6. The descent of the Holy Spirit recalls the dove in Noah's story, symbolizing peace, and a new beginning. How does baptism symbolize a fresh start in your spiritual life?
7. Matthew 3:13-17 gives a glimpse of the Trinity working in unity. How does this scene shape your understanding of the relationship between the Father, Son, and Holy Spirit?
8. Jesus's baptism marked the beginning of His public ministry. In what ways does your baptism or commitment to Christ inspire you to serve others and share the Gospel?
9. Paul writes in Galatians 3:26-29 that through baptism, we become united as God's family. How can we live out this unity and love in our church and community?
10. Reflecting on Jesus's baptism, what steps can you take to deepen your trust in God's plan for your life, even when it requires humility and sacrifice?

Chapter 2

1. Why do you think Jesus spent an entire night in prayer before choosing the twelve apostles? How does this emphasize the importance of seeking God's guidance in decision-making?
2. The apostles came from diverse backgrounds, including fishermen and a tax collector. What does this diversity tell us about God's Kingdom and His call for people?
3. Peter was named "the rock" by Jesus, symbolizing his role in building the Church. How does God's calling in your life shape your identity and purpose?
4. Judas Iscariot, who betrayed Jesus, was included in the twelve. What lessons can we learn about free will and responsibility from his inclusion?
5. Paul writes in 1 Corinthians 1:26-29 that God often chooses the weak and ordinary to display His power. How does this encourage you in your walk of faith?
6. The apostles were chosen not for their skills but for their willingness to follow Jesus. What does this teach us about the kind of people God calls to serve Him?
7. Gideon's story (Judges 6) shows that God often calls unlikely people for great tasks. Can you think of a time when God used your weaknesses to accomplish something significant?
8. Paul explains in Romans 12 and 1 Corinthians 12 that believers are given unique spiritual gifts. How can discovering and using your spiritual gifts strengthen your role in the church and your community?
9. Jesus's method of selecting and training the apostles involved close relationship and discipleship. How can this model shape the way we mentor or lead others in our faith communities?

10. The apostles were chosen to "teach, preach, and perform miracles in Jesus' name." How can we, as modern disciples, live out this mission in our daily lives?

Chapter 3

1. John the Baptist declared that his baptism was with water, but that Jesus would baptize with the Holy Spirit and fire. What do you think it means to be baptized with the Holy Spirit? How has this been evident in your life?
2. Luke 3:16 shows John's humility when he says he is not worthy to untie Jesus' sandals. How can we cultivate humility in our own calling and ministry?
3. John's message prepared people's hearts for Jesus. In what ways can we prepare others to encounter Christ in their lives today?
4. The Holy Spirit plays a central role in transforming believers. According to Galatians 5:22-23, what are some ways the Spirit's work is visible in a person's life?
5. John boldly fulfilled his role, even though it meant he wasn't the center of attention. How can we embrace God's purpose for us without seeking personal recognition?
6. Luke 3:16 mentions fire as a part of the Spirit's work. How do you understand the refining and cleansing work of the Holy Spirit in your spiritual growth?
7. John's calling mirrors that of Elijah, boldly calling people to repentance. Have you ever felt called to speak boldly for God? What challenges did you face, and how did you respond?
8. John pointed people to Jesus and not himself. How can we ensure that our actions and words direct others to Christ and not just to us?
9. The Spirit empowers believers for witness (Acts 1:8). How can we rely on the Holy Spirit to share our faith with others more effectively?
10. Luke 3:16 reminds us of the Holy Spirit's constant presence in our lives. How does this assurance give you courage and peace as you live out your faith daily?

Chapter 4

1. John 3:16 begins with "For God so loved the world." What does this tell us about the depth and breadth of God's love, and how does it challenge our understanding of love?
2. 2. Why do you think Jesus emphasizes faith as the key to salvation? How does putting faith in Him transform the way we live?
3. 3. John 3:16 describes Jesus as God's ultimate gift. How can recognizing Jesus as a gift change the way we view our relationship with God and with others?
4. 4. Eternal life is promised to those who believe in Jesus. What does "eternal life" mean to you, and how does it shape your perspective on earthly challenges?
5. 5. Nicodemus comes to Jesus at night, seeking answers. What does his journey teach us about seeking truth, even when we have doubts or fears?
6. 6. Romans 5:8 says, "While we were still sinners, Christ died for us." How does this truth impact the way we view God's love and grace in our own lives?
7. 7. In what ways does the message of John 3:16 inspire you to share the Gospel with others? How can you make this message accessible to those who haven't heard it?
8. 8. Jesus speaks of being "born again" to Nicodemus. What does spiritual rebirth mean to you, and how have you experienced it in your faith journey?
9. 9. Nicodemus' transformation from curiosity to faith is gradual. What lessons can we learn from his story about patience and persistence in sharing our faith with others?
10. 10. John 3:16 offers hope and assurance. How can this verse encourage us in times of doubt or fear, and how can we use it to encourage others?

Chapter 5

1. Peter and John gave the crippled man something more valuable than money—healing through faith in Jesus. What can we offer to others when we feel we have little to give?
2. In Acts 3:16, Peter emphasizes that the healing was through faith in the name of Jesus. What does this teach us about the power and authority of Jesus' name in our own lives?
3. The crippled man had been at the temple gate for years, but this time he experienced transformation. Why do you think faith and timing played such significant roles in his healing?
4. When the man was healed, he immediately began walking, jumping, and praising God. How do you express gratitude and joy for God's work in your life?
5. Peter and John acted boldly in faith when they healed the man. What steps can you take to live with boldness and faith in your everyday life?
6. The healing drew a crowd, and Peter used the opportunity to preach repentance. How can we use moments in our lives to point others to Jesus?
7. Isaiah 35:6 prophesied that the lame would leap like a deer. How does seeing God's promises fulfilled in Scripture strengthen your faith?
8. The healing restored the man not only physically but also socially and spiritually. How does God's work in your life bring restoration in different areas?
9. The Roman centurion's faith in Matthew 8:8 mirrors the faith shown in Acts 3:16. What can we learn from these examples about trusting Jesus' authority, even when we can't see the outcome?

10. Peter attributed the healing to Jesus, not his own power. How can we remain humble and give God the glory for what He accomplishes through us?

Chapter 6

1. Romans 3:16 describes the consequences of sin as "ruin and misery." How have you seen these effects of sin in your own life or in the world around you?
2. Paul highlights the universal nature of sin in Romans 3. How does understanding that "all have sinned" (Romans 3:23) shape your view of yourself and others?
3. King Saul's story in 1 Samuel illustrates the ruin caused by disobedience. What lessons can we learn from Saul's failure to fully follow God's will?
4. Although Romans 3 paints a bleak picture of humanity's condition, it points to the hope of grace through Jesus. How does this tension between sin and grace impact your understanding of God's love?
5. Paul emphasizes that outward actions alone are not enough—God desires a faithful heart. How can we focus more on inward transformation rather than outward appearances in our walk with God?
6. Romans 5:8 reminds us that Christ died for us while we were still sinners. How does this truth inspire gratitude and humility in your relationship with God?
7. The ruin and misery of sin can also affect our relationships. How can we actively seek reconciliation and restoration through God's grace?
8. In 2 Corinthians 5:17, Paul describes believers as new creations in Christ. What does it mean to you to live as a "new creation"?
9. Peter's question about forgiveness in Matthew 18:21-22 highlights the importance of showing grace to others. How can we reflect God's forgiveness in our daily interactions?
10. Romans 3:16 reminds us of the devastating effects of sin, but also of the hope in Christ's redemption. How can we share this

message of both warning and hope with others in a way that resonates with them?

Chapter 7

1. Paul describes the church as God's temple, where the Spirit of God dwells. How does this understanding impact the way we view and treat our church community?
2. The Corinthians struggled with division, following human leaders rather than Christ. What are some ways modern churches can avoid similar divisions and remain united in Christ?
3. Paul warns about building the church with lasting materials like "gold, silver, and costly stones." What does it look like to build a church with these "materials" today?
4. 1 Corinthians 3:16 emphasizes the sacredness of the church as God's temple. How can we ensure our words and actions build up the church rather than harm it?
5. Paul contrasts worldly behavior with spiritual growth. How can we identify areas where we may still be conforming to worldly patterns, and how can we pursue spiritual maturity?
6. Daniel is an example of someone who lived as a temple of God, remaining faithful and holy in a hostile environment. What practical steps can we take to reflect God's holiness in our daily lives?
7. The Old Testament temple was a physical place where God's presence dwelled. How does the shift to God dwelling in His people through the Spirit change our understanding of worship and community?
8. Jesus is described as the cornerstone of the temple in Matthew 21:42. How can we ensure that Jesus remains the foundation of our personal and corporate spiritual lives?
9. Paul reminds us of the serious consequences of defiling God's temple. How can we guard against attitudes or actions that might harm the church community?

10. Romans 12:2 calls us not to conform to the world but to be transformed by the renewing of our minds. How can we renew our minds daily to live as temples of the Holy Spirit?

Chapter 8

1. Paul contrasts the old covenant with the new covenant in 2 Corinthians 3. How does understanding this contrast deepen your appreciation for what Christ has done for us?
2. The veil Moses wore symbolized separation from God's full glory. What "veils" might we have in our lives today that prevent us from fully experiencing God's presence?
3. Paul writes that "whenever anyone turns to the Lord, the veil is taken away" (2 Corinthians 3:16). How have you experienced spiritual transformation after turning to Christ?
4. The Holy Spirit plays a key role in unveiling truth and transforming believers. How do you actively rely on the Holy Spirit to guide your spiritual growth?
5. Josiah's story in 2 Kings 22 illustrates the removal of spiritual blindness. How can his example inspire us to respond when God reveals areas of sin or neglect in our lives?
6. Paul describes the new covenant as bringing righteousness and life. How does this understanding impact the way you live out your faith?
7. In 2 Corinthians 3:18, Paul speaks of being transformed "from glory to glory." What does this process of transformation look like in your daily life?
8. The psalmist prays in Psalm 119:18, "Open my eyes that I may see wonderful things in your law." How can we cultivate a posture of openness to God's truth?
9. Paul suggests that spiritual blindness can obscure our view of Christ. What practical steps can we take to remove distractions or barriers that keep us from seeing His glory?
10. The unveiled glory of Christ allows believers to reflect His image to others. How can we ensure that our lives reflect His character and love in a way that draws others to Him?

Chapter 9

1. Paul emphasizes that God's promise to Abraham referred to a singular "seed," Christ. How does this understanding deepen your appreciation for Jesus' role in God's plan of salvation?
2. Why do you think Paul found it so important to clarify the difference between salvation by faith and salvation through the law? How does this apply to believers today?
3. Paul connects Abraham's faith with righteousness. How does Abraham's example challenge or encourage you in your own faith journey?
4. Galatians 3:16 highlights Jesus as the fulfillment of God's promise. How does knowing this impact your perspective on God's faithfulness to His promises?
5. In John 14:6, Jesus declares that He is the only way to the Father. How does this exclusivity of Christ shape your approach to sharing the Gospel with others?
6. David's covenant in 2 Samuel 7 points to Christ as the eternal King. How does the connection between these covenants demonstrate the unity and consistency of God's plan throughout Scripture?
7. Paul contrasts the law, which reveals sin, with faith in Christ, which brings salvation. How can we balance understanding the importance of God's law while fully relying on grace?
8. Faith in Jesus brings transformation and spiritual growth. How have you experienced this transformation in your own life, and how can you help others recognize it in theirs?
9. The Galatian church struggled with relying on works instead of faith. What modern challenges might Christians face in trusting solely in Christ for salvation?

10. David's lineage culminates in Christ, fulfilling God's promise to establish an eternal kingdom. How does this inspire trust in God's long-term plan for your life and His world?

Chapter 10

1. Paul prays for believers to be strengthened in their inner being through the Spirit. How does this inner strength empower you to face challenges in your spiritual journey?
2. What does it mean to you to be "rooted and established in love"? How does this foundation influence your daily decisions and interactions?
3. Paul connects spiritual strength with the Holy Spirit's work within us. How have you experienced the Spirit strengthening you in difficult times?
4. Nehemiah relied on God's strength to rebuild Jerusalem's walls despite opposition. What lessons can we learn from his faith and perseverance for our own challenges?
5. Paul describes God's grace as "glorious riches." How does understanding the abundance of God's grace impact your perspective on His provision for your needs?
6. Being "rooted in love" transforms relationships. How does living in God's love shape the way you interact with family, friends, and those in your community?
7. Paul's prayer invites believers to explore the depth of God's love. How can you intentionally grow in your understanding and experience of His love?
8. Colossians 2:6-7 speaks of being "rooted and built up in Him." How do spiritual disciplines like prayer and studying Scripture help you stay firmly rooted in your faith?
9. Ephesians 3:16 emphasizes that true strength comes from God, not us. How can we surrender areas of self-reliance and allow God's Spirit to work through us?
10. Paul ends this section of his prayer with a doxology of praise (Ephesians 3:20-21). How does praising God for His power and love encourage you in your walk with Him?

Chapter 11

1. Paul encourages believers to "live up to what we have already attained." What does it mean to you to live in alignment with the spiritual growth you've already experienced?
2. Paul compares the Christian life to a race. What "goals" do you set in your spiritual life, and how do you keep your focus on Christ as the ultimate prize?
3. In Philippians 3:12-13, Paul admits he has not yet achieved perfection. How does this humility inspire you to view your own spiritual journey?
4. Ruth demonstrated perseverance and steadfast faith in her journey with Naomi. How does her story encourage you to press on in difficult circumstances?
5. Paul emphasizes the importance of Christian fellowship. How can you build deeper relationships with others in your church community to encourage spiritual growth?
6. Hebrews 6:1 calls believers to move toward maturity. What practical steps can you take to grow in wisdom, discernment, and the fruit of the Spirit in your daily life?
7. Paul tells believers to observe and imitate godly examples. Who in your life has been a spiritual role model, and how has their example influenced your faith?
8. Christian fellowship often involves carrying one another's burdens (Galatians 6:2). How can we support each other better in our shared spiritual journey?
9. Ruth left behind her old life to embrace faith in God. Are there areas in your life where you need to let go of the past to grow spiritually?
10. Paul calls for unity among believers as they press toward the goal together. How can we foster unity within our small group

or church community to better reflect Christ's love to the world?

Chapter 12

1. Paul calls believers to let the Word of Christ dwell richly among them. How do you ensure that God's Word is a central part of your daily life?
2. Colossians 3:16 emphasizes teaching and admonishing one another with wisdom. How can we balance encouragement and accountability within our Christian community?
3. Paul highlights worship through psalms, hymns, and spiritual songs. How does worship impact your relationship with God and your sense of unity with other believers?
4. Ezra's dedication to teaching God's Word led to a communal renewal in Nehemiah 8. How can we create opportunities in our church or small group for collective engagement with Scripture?
5. Paul contrasts the "old self" with the "new self" in Colossians 3. What old attitudes or behaviors might you need to "put off," and what virtues can you "put on" to reflect Christ more fully?
6. Proverbs 27:17 says, "As iron sharpens iron, so one person sharpens another." How can you be intentional about sharpening and being sharpened by others in your faith journey?
7. Colossians 3:16 encourages gratitude to flow from a deep understanding of God's Word. How has engaging in Scripture led to a greater sense of thankfulness in your life?
8. Paul describes the transformative power of Scripture in shaping both individuals and the community. What steps can we take to allow God's Word to influence our thoughts, decisions, and actions more profoundly?
9. Worship is both personal and communal. How can we ensure that our times of worship are more than routine, becoming opportunities for genuine connection with God and others?

10. Joshua 1:8 encourages meditating on God's Word day and night. What practical ways can you make Scripture meditation a consistent and impactful part of your spiritual growth?

Chapter 13

1. Paul expresses his gratitude for the Thessalonians' faith and perseverance. How can gratitude for the faith of others strengthen your own spiritual walk?
2. The Thessalonians endured trials and persecution but remained faithful. What challenges do you face in living out your faith, and how do you stay encouraged?
3. Paul urges believers to live with holiness and purpose in light of Christ's return. How does keeping eternity in view influence your daily decisions and priorities?
4. Hannah's persistent prayer in 1 Samuel mirrors Paul's call to "pray continually." How can a lifestyle of continual prayer deepen your relationship with God?
5. Paul emphasizes the importance of Christian fellowship and accountability. How can we foster stronger connections within our small group or church community?
6. Paul compares his care for the Thessalonians to that of a nursing mother. How does this imagery challenge or inspire the way you care for others in your faith community?
7. 1 Thessalonians 5:16-18 encourages believers to "rejoice always, pray continually, give thanks in all circumstances." How do you practice gratitude and joy even during difficult times?
8. The anticipation of Christ's return motivated the Thessalonians to live faithfully. How can reflecting on this future hope shape your response to current struggles or uncertainties?
9. Paul highlights faith, hope, and love as central themes for the Christian life. Which of these do you find most challenging, and how can you grow in that area?
10. Romans 8:18 reminds us that present sufferings are temporary compared to future glory. How does this truth help you endure trials and encourage others in their faith journey?

Chapter 14

1. Paul prays for the Lord of peace to give peace "at all times and in every way." How have you experienced God's peace in challenging or uncertain times?
2. The Thessalonians faced anxiety and division due to false teachings. How can we guard against confusion and remain grounded in God's truth today?
3. Paul's blessing of peace extends to the entire church, emphasizing unity. How can our church or small group foster a deeper sense of harmony and shared purpose?
4. Hezekiah sought peace by turning to God in prayer during the Assyrian siege. How can prayer help us respond to threats or challenges in our lives with trust rather than panic?
5. Paul encourages believers to stand firm and continue doing what is right. What does perseverance in faith look like in your life, especially during difficult circumstances?
6. The biblical concept of shalom encompasses wholeness and well-being. How can we seek and share this kind of peace with others in our community?
7. Paul addresses idleness and anxiety among the Thessalonians. How can we strike a balance between trusting God's plan and actively living out our faith?
8. Isaiah 26:3 promises perfect peace to those who trust in God. What practical steps can we take to keep our minds steadfastly focused on Him?
9. Hezekiah laid his fears before God in the temple. What does it look like for you to lay your burdens before God, and how has that brought peace to your heart?
10. Paul ends his letter by focusing on God's grace and peace. How can we bring God's peace into our relationships, workplaces, and everyday interactions with others?

Chapter 15

1. Paul describes the "mystery of godliness" as being revealed in Jesus Christ. How does this understanding deepen your appreciation of the gospel?
2. "He appeared in the flesh" highlights Jesus' humanity and divinity. How does Jesus' incarnation impact your relationship with Him and your understanding of God's love?
3. "Vindicated by the Spirit" refers to the Holy Spirit affirming Jesus' ministry. How do you see the Holy Spirit working in your life today to confirm your faith?
4. Angels were present at key moments in Jesus' life, such as His birth, resurrection, and ascension. What does their role teach us about God's divine plan and His care for humanity?
5. "Taken up in glory" points to Jesus' ascension and His reign. How does the knowledge that Jesus is interceding for you at God's right hand encourage you in your daily life?
6. Samuel exemplified a life of godliness and obedience to God's calling. What steps can we take to live with similar devotion and humility?
7. 1 Timothy 3:16 emphasizes the core truths of the gospel. How can we share these truths with clarity and boldness in our everyday conversations?
8. Paul's description of Jesus' life, death, and exaltation calls believers to reflect His humility and sacrificial love. How can we demonstrate this love in our relationships and communities?
9. The mystery of godliness points toward God's redemptive plan. How does this truth inspire you to live with hope and anticipation for Christ's return?
10. Micah 6:8 calls us to act justly, love mercy, and walk humbly with God. How can these values guide us in living out the truths described in 1 Timothy 3:16?

Chapter 16

1. Paul describes all Scripture as "God-breathed." How does understanding the divine origin of the Bible impact the way you read and apply it in your life?
2. 2 Timothy 3:16 highlights four purposes of Scripture: teaching, rebuking, correcting, and training in righteousness. Which of these do you find most impactful in your spiritual growth, and why?
3. Apollos demonstrated humility when Priscilla and Aquila corrected his teaching. How can we remain open to correction and growth in our understanding of Scripture?
4. Paul emphasizes that Scripture equips believers for every good work (2 Timothy 3:17). How has God's Word equipped you for a specific challenge or opportunity in your life?
5. Matthew 4:4 says, "Man shall not live on bread alone, but on every word that comes from the mouth of God." How can we cultivate a deeper dependence on Scripture for spiritual nourishment?
6. Paul wrote to encourage Timothy in the face of false teachings. How can consistent engagement with Scripture help us discern truth from error in today's world?
7. Joshua 1:8 urges believers to meditate on God's Word day and night. What practical steps can you take to make Scripture meditation a consistent part of your daily routine?
8. The Bible reveals God's character, will, and plan for salvation. What aspect of God's nature has been most clear to you through your study of Scripture?
9. 2 Peter 1:21 emphasizes that prophecy originates from God, not human will. How does this truth enhance your trust in the authority and reliability of the Bible?

10. Apollos used Scripture to boldly proclaim Jesus as the Messiah. How can we effectively use God's Word to share the gospel and encourage others in their faith?

Chapter 17

1. Paul emphasized the importance of appointing elders with specific qualities in Titus 1. What qualities do you think are most essential for leaders in today's church, and why?
2. Paul calls for sound doctrine to be taught and defended. How can we ensure that our church remains rooted in the truth of the gospel in a world full of competing messages?
3. In Titus 2:14, Paul speaks of Jesus redeeming a people "eager to do what is good." How can good works serve as evidence of our faith and a witness to the world?
4. Barnabas exemplified encouragement and mentorship. How can we follow his example by encouraging and mentoring others in their faith journey?
5. Paul warns Titus about false teachers and divisive people. How can we lovingly correct those who stray from sound doctrine while maintaining unity in the church?
6. Paul connects grace with godly living in Titus 2. How does understanding God's grace inspire you to live a life that reflects righteousness and love for others?
7. In Titus 3:14, Paul reminds believers to devote themselves to doing good. What are some practical ways you can live out your faith through acts of service and kindness?
8. Paul instructs Titus to teach sound doctrine that transforms lives. How has Scripture transformed your life, and how can you use it to encourage others in their walk with Christ?
9. Barnabas gave John Mark a second chance despite his earlier failure. How can we show grace and restoration to those who have fallen short but desire to grow in their faith?
10. Paul emphasizes that godly leadership requires integrity and humility. How can we cultivate these qualities in our leadership roles, whether in the church, workplace, or home?

Chapter 18

1. Paul appeals to Philemon in love rather than commanding him to forgive Onesimus. How does this approach demonstrate the power of love in reconciliation?
2. Paul urges Philemon to see Onesimus not as a slave but as a brother in Christ. How does the gospel challenge societal or personal barriers in your relationships?
3. Forgiveness and reconciliation are central themes in this letter. How have you experienced the transforming power of forgiveness in your own life?
4. Paul describes Philemon's faith and love as encouraging and refreshing to others. How can we, as Christians, reflect these qualities in our daily interactions?
5. Paul offers to repay any debt Onesimus owes. What does this teach us about sacrificial love and the cost of reconciliation?
6. Jonathan's relationship with David exemplifies sacrificial love and peacemaking. How can we follow Jonathan's example in resolving conflicts or supporting others in need?
7. Paul's letter encourages seeing people through the lens of grace rather than their past actions. How can this perspective transform how we treat those who have wronged us?
8. Proverbs 17:17 says, "A friend loves at all times, and a brother is born for a time of adversity." How can we demonstrate loyalty and love to those in our community who are struggling?
9. In Ephesians 4:32, Paul urges believers to forgive as God forgave them. How does reflecting on God's forgiveness help you extend grace to others?
10. Paul's letter calls for a radical kind of reconciliation rooted in the gospel. How can we model this kind of grace and forgiveness in our families, workplaces, and communities?

Chapter 19

1. The Israelites witnessed God's miracles but still rebelled in unbelief. How does this challenge you to reflect on areas of your life where you might struggle to trust God?
2. Hebrews 3:16 serves as a warning against rebellion. How can regular self-examination help us stay faithful in our walk with Christ?
3. Caleb trusted God's promises, even when others doubted. What lessons can we learn from his faith and courage in the face of opposition?
4. The writer of Hebrews draws a parallel between the Israelites' rebellion and the temptations Christians face today. What modern "wilderness" experiences test your faith, and how do you overcome them?
5. Jesus resisted temptation in the wilderness by relying on Scripture. How can knowing and applying God's Word help you stand firm against temptation?
6. Unbelief kept the Israelites from entering God's rest. How does this motivate you to persevere in faith, especially during difficult times?
7. Adam and Eve, the Israelites, and the audience of Hebrews all faced the consequences of unbelief. How does their example shape the way you approach challenges in your own faith?
8. Hebrews 12:1-2 calls believers to fix their eyes on Jesus and run with perseverance. What practical steps can you take to keep your focus on Christ in your daily life?
9. 1 John 2:16 warns against loving the things of the world. How can we guard our hearts against distractions that pull us away from our faith?

10. The message of Hebrews 3:16 emphasizes faith as a lifelong commitment. How can Christian community and accountability help us remain steadfast in our journey of faith?

Chapter 20

1. James contrasts heavenly wisdom with earthly wisdom. How do you distinguish between the two in your daily decisions and interactions?
2. James warns that envy and selfish ambition lead to disorder and evil practices. How have you seen these traits negatively impact relationships or communities, and how can they be avoided?
3. Heavenly wisdom is described as pure, peace-loving, and full of mercy. How can these qualities shape the way you approach conflict or disagreements?
4. James compares the tongue to a small spark that can start a large fire. How can we better control our words to reflect godly wisdom rather than earthly tendencies?
5. Diotrephes in 3 John serves as a warning against selfish ambition. What lessons can we learn from his actions about humility and servant leadership?
6. Proverbs 14:12 warns about paths that seem right but lead to death. How can we ensure we are pursuing wisdom that aligns with God's will rather than worldly values?
7. Philippians 2:3-4 emphasizes humility and valuing others above us. How can practicing these principles foster unity within your small group or church community?
8. James highlights the importance of actions that reflect true wisdom. What practical steps can you take to ensure your deeds align with your faith?
9. Earthly wisdom often prioritizes personal gain, while heavenly wisdom seeks to serve others. How can you shift your focus from self-centered goals to Christ-centered purposes?
10. Colossians 3:17 encourages believers to do everything in the name of Jesus with gratitude. How can this mindset transform the way you approach both ordinary tasks and major decisions?

Chapter 21

1. Peter encourages believers to maintain a clear conscience. How can we ensure that our actions and words align with our faith, even in challenging situations?
2. Peter calls Christians to respond to hostility with gentleness and respect. What does this look like in practical terms, especially in today's culture?
3. Stephen demonstrated boldness and grace in the face of persecution. How can his example inspire us to stand firm in our faith when we face opposition?
4. Peter emphasizes being ready to give an answer for the hope we have in Christ. How can we prepare ourselves to share our faith effectively and confidently?
5. Peter's teaching reflects Jesus' command to love our enemies. How can we demonstrate Christ-like love toward those who criticize or misunderstand our beliefs?
6. 1 Peter 1:4 speaks of an inheritance that will never perish. How does this eternal perspective encourage you to persevere through trials or hostility?
7. Peter describes believers as living stones in a spiritual house. How can we support and encourage one another as part of a united community of faith?
8. Isaiah 8:13 reminds us to regard the Lord as holy and trust Him fully. How does honoring Christ as Lord in your heart strengthen your faith during difficult times?
9. Peter acknowledges that suffering for doing good is sometimes unavoidable. How can we find peace and joy in Christ, even when facing adversity?
10. Stephen's prayer for his persecutors mirrored Jesus' forgiveness on the cross. How can we cultivate a heart of forgiveness and grace toward those who oppose us?

Chapter 22

1. Peter warns against distorting Scripture. How can we ensure that our interpretation of the Bible remains faithful to its intended meaning?
2. Peter acknowledges that Paul's letters can be difficult to understand. How can we approach challenging passages of Scripture with humility and a desire to learn?
3. The Bereans in Acts 17 examined Scripture daily to verify truth. How can we adopt a similar discipline in our personal Bible study and spiritual growth?
4. False teachings are a recurring theme in 2 Peter. What are some modern examples of teachings that may distort Scripture, and how can we guard against them?
5. Peter emphasizes spiritual growth as a safeguard against falsehood. What steps can you take to grow in your faith and deepen your understanding of God's Word?
6. Philip the Evangelist helped the Ethiopian eunuch understand Scripture. How can we help others grasp the truth of the Bible and apply it to their lives?
7. Proverbs 4:7 highlights the value of wisdom and understanding. How do we prioritize seeking wisdom from Scripture in our daily routines and decision-making?
8. Peter's acknowledgment of Paul's letters as Scripture underscores the unity of the Bible. How does viewing Scripture as a unified whole impact your understanding of God's plan?
9. 2 Timothy 3:16 reminds us that all Scripture is God-breathed and useful. How has Scripture personally guided, corrected, or encouraged you in your walk with Christ?
10. Peter's life exemplifies boldness in defending truth. How can we stand firm in our faith and share biblical truth with gentleness and respect in today's culture?

Chapter 23

1. 1 John 3:16 defines love through Jesus' sacrifice. How does this example challenge or inspire you to love others more selflessly?
2. John urges believers to lay down their lives for others. What does sacrificial love look like in your daily life, and how can you live it out practically?
3. Joseph of Arimathea demonstrated courageous love in caring for Jesus' body. What risks or sacrifices might be involved in showing Christ-like love in your life?
4. John emphasizes love as the heart of God's message. How can prioritizing love strengthen relationships within your church or community?
5. Jesus' love transcended social and cultural barriers. How can we, as believers, reflect this inclusive and unconditional love in a divided world?
6. 1 John contrasts light and darkness, calling believers to walk in the light. What steps can you take to remain in the light of Christ in challenging circumstances?
7. Love in action is a recurring theme in Scripture. What are some practical ways you can show love to others beyond just words?
8. John highlights unity within the body of Christ. How does sacrificial love contribute to building a diverse yet united Christian community?
9. Galatians 3:28 speaks of being "one in Christ." How can we break down barriers in our own lives to reflect this unity in our relationships?
10. At the core of Christianity is God's love for humanity. How does reflecting on God's love for you personally transform the way you love others?

Chapter 24

1. John emphasizes the inseparability of truth and love. How can you balance these two qualities in your interactions with others, especially during disagreements?
2. John calls believers to "walk in truth" by obeying God's commands. What does walking in truth look like in your daily life, and how can you stay grounded in God's Word?
3. The letter warns against welcoming false teachers. How can we practice discernment while still being loving and welcoming to those who may not share our beliefs?
4. Priscilla and Aquila exemplified balancing truth and love when teaching Apollos. How can you lovingly correct or guide someone who misunderstands or misrepresents the gospel?
5. In a world of shifting morals and values, how can Christians ensure they remain aligned with biblical truth without compromising love and compassion?
6. John encourages the recipients to hold firmly to Jesus' teachings. What specific practices or habits can help you grow in understanding and applying biblical truth?
7. Matthew 5:44 calls us to love our enemies. How can you extend love to those who oppose your beliefs without compromising the truth of the gospel?
8. John's letter highlights the importance of Christian unity. How does truth and love within the church serve as a witness to the world around us?
9. What challenges have you faced when trying to live out both truth and love in your relationships, and how can John's message help you navigate those situations?
10. Jesus prayed, "Sanctify them by the truth; your word is truth" (John 17:17). How can you use Scripture as a guide to test teachings, values, or practices in today's culture?

Chapter 25

1. Gaius is commended for walking in truth. What does "walking in truth" look like in your daily life, and how can it impact others around you?
2. Hospitality is a central theme in 3 John. How can we practice hospitality today, both in our homes and within our church communities?
3. John links truth with love repeatedly in his letters. How can we ensure that our pursuit of truth is always accompanied by love and humility?
4. Diotrephes is described as someone who "loves to be first." How can pride hinder our ability to serve others and practice hospitality?
5. John emphasizes supporting those who "go out for the sake of the Name." How can we better support missionaries, teachers, and those serving in ministry today?
6. Cornelius in Acts 10 demonstrates both hospitality and openness to God's truth. How does his story inspire you to welcome others and share the gospel?
7. How can we balance being welcoming and hospitable with exercising discernment about who we support, as John advises in verse 10?
8. Proverbs 16:18 warns against pride leading to destruction. What steps can we take to guard our hearts against pride in our relationships and service to others?
9. John's letter contrasts the humility of Gaius with the pride of Diotrephes. How can we ensure our actions reflect Gaius' spirit of generosity and support for others?
10. In what ways can practicing hospitality be a witness to the gospel in a world that often values individualism over community?

Chapter 26

1. Jude urges believers to "contend for the faith" (verse 3). What does this look like in our daily lives, and how can we balance standing firmly with showing love and grace?
2. Jude provides several Old Testament examples of rebellion and judgment (e.g., Cain, Balaam, Korah). How do these stories help us understand the dangers of straying from God's truth?
3. False teachers are described as distorting grace and promoting ungodly living (verse 4). What are some modern examples of distorted teachings, and how can we discern truth from error?
4. Jude emphasizes spiritual vigilance through practices like prayer, building faith, and keeping in God's love (verses 20-21). How can we incorporate these habits into our lives to strengthen our faith?
5. How do we show mercy to those who doubt or struggle with their faith (verses 22-23), while also guarding ourselves from being influenced by sin?
6. Phinehas acted zealously to protect Israel from sin in Numbers 25. How can we balance zeal for God's truth with humility and compassion in today's context?
7. Jude warns against pride, greed, and rebellion, as seen in the examples of Cain, Balaam, and Korah. How can we guard our hearts against these attitudes in our own lives?
8. In verse 7, Jude references Sodom and Gomorrah to emphasize the consequences of ungodly living. How can we address issues of morality in our culture without becoming judgmental or self-righteous?
9. What role does accountability within the Christian community play in helping us contend for the faith and avoid false teachings?

10. Jude concludes his letter with a doxology praising God for His power to keep believers from stumbling (verses 24-25). How does this promise encourage us when facing challenges to our faith?

Chapter 27

1. Jesus describes the Laodicean church as "lukewarm." How would you define spiritual lukewarmness in today's context, and what are some signs of it in your own life or church?
2. The Laodiceans were self-reliant due to their wealth and resources. How can material prosperity hinder our dependence on God, and how do we guard against this?
3. Jesus says, "I am about to spit you out of my mouth." Why do you think lukewarm faith is so offensive to God compared to being cold or hot?
4. What does it mean to be "hot" or "cold" in the context of faith? How can these states reflect a healthy spiritual life?
5. King Amaziah's story in 2 Chronicles 25:2 highlights half-hearted devotion. How does his life serve as a warning for Christians about the dangers of partial obedience to God?
6. In what ways can prayer, study, worship, and serving others help us move from lukewarm faith to a deeper relationship with Christ? Which of these practices do you need to prioritize?
7. Jesus extends an invitation to the Laodiceans in verse 20, saying, "Here I am! I stand at the door and knock." How can we ensure that our hearts remain open to Jesus, especially in times of spiritual complacency?
8. What role does community and accountability play in helping us avoid spiritual lukewarmness? How can we encourage one another to stay "on fire" for God?
9. Jesus identifies Himself as the "faithful and true witness" at the beginning of the letter. How does reflecting on Jesus' faithfulness inspire us to remain steadfast and zealous in our faith?
10. The letter to Laodicea ends with a promise to those who overcome: to sit with Jesus on His throne (verse 21). How does this

promise motivate you to remain spiritually fervent and committed to following Christ?

www.ingramcontent.com/pod-product-compliance
Lightning Source LLC
LaVergne TN
LVHW010216070526
838199LV00062B/4616